Lynne Pickering
Art and Interiors

Feng Shui Decor
Book three Series

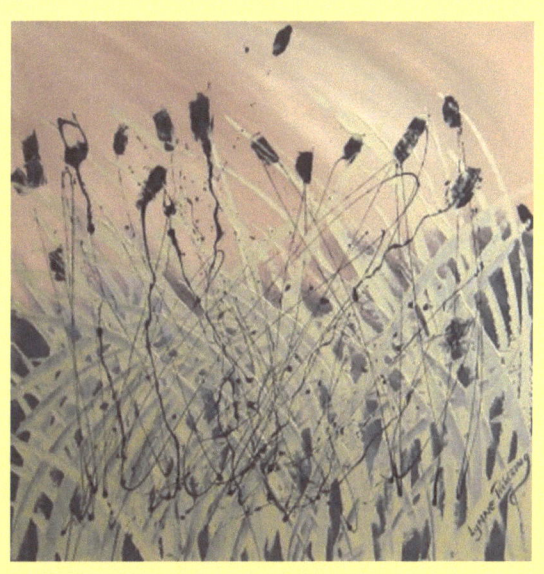

ISBN:1516922867

ISBN-13:978-1516922864

DEDICATION

This is a representative selection of the art over 5,500 paintings I have sold in over 32 countries. I want to thank my husband for his expert packing and care taken for the art to arrive in pristine condition , and to my many patrons who have my art in their home, or commercial buildings, art galleries, castles, apartments and Law Chambers and many café's and restaurants.

CONTENTS

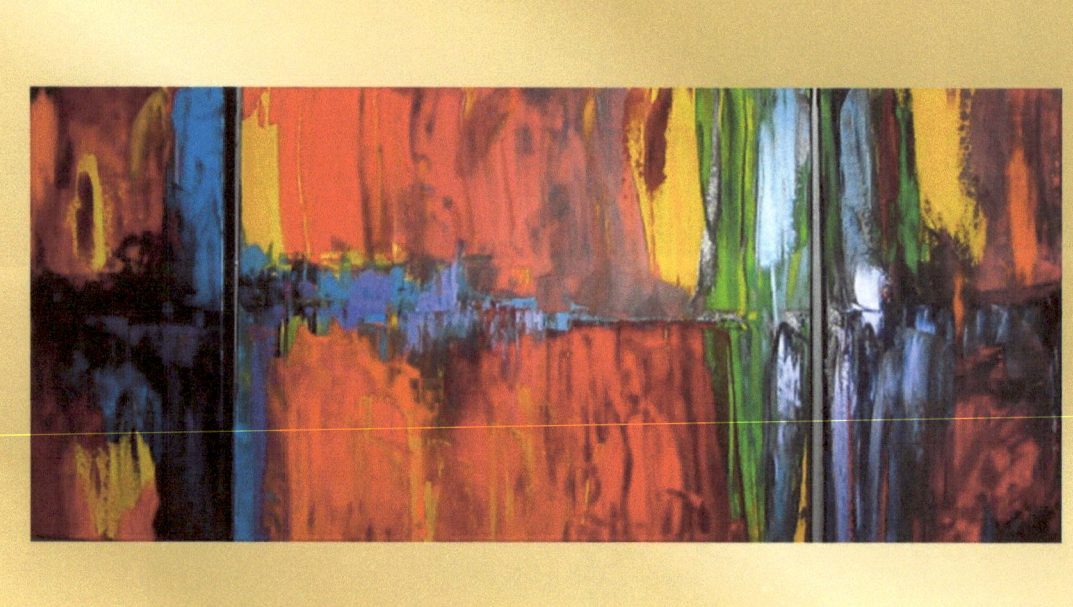

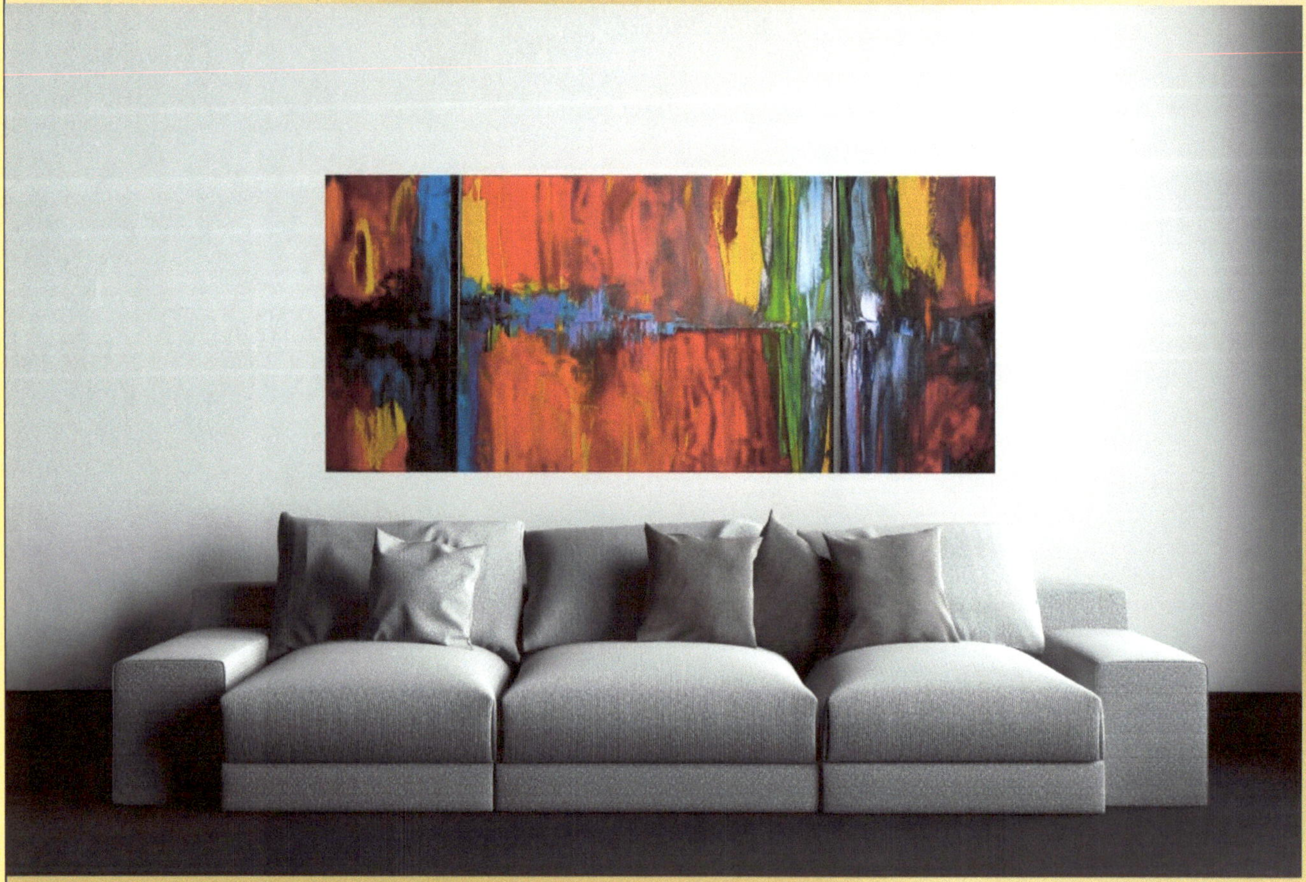

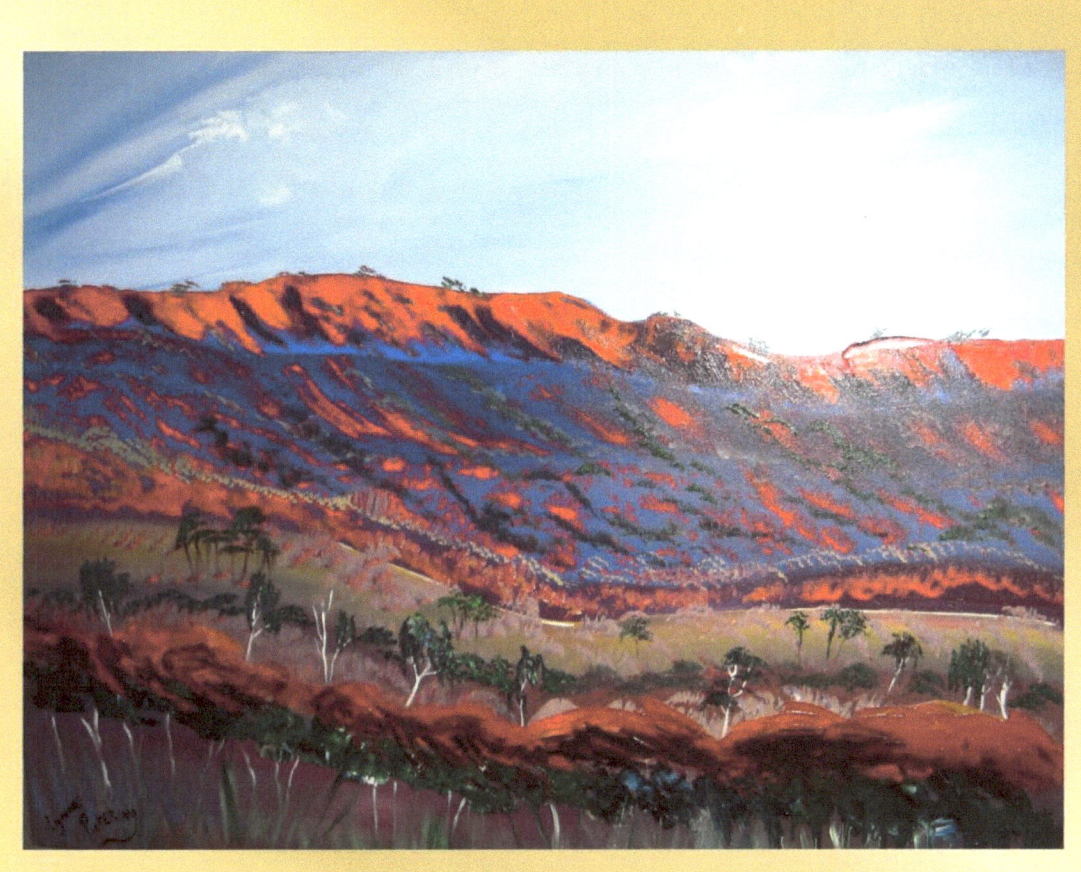

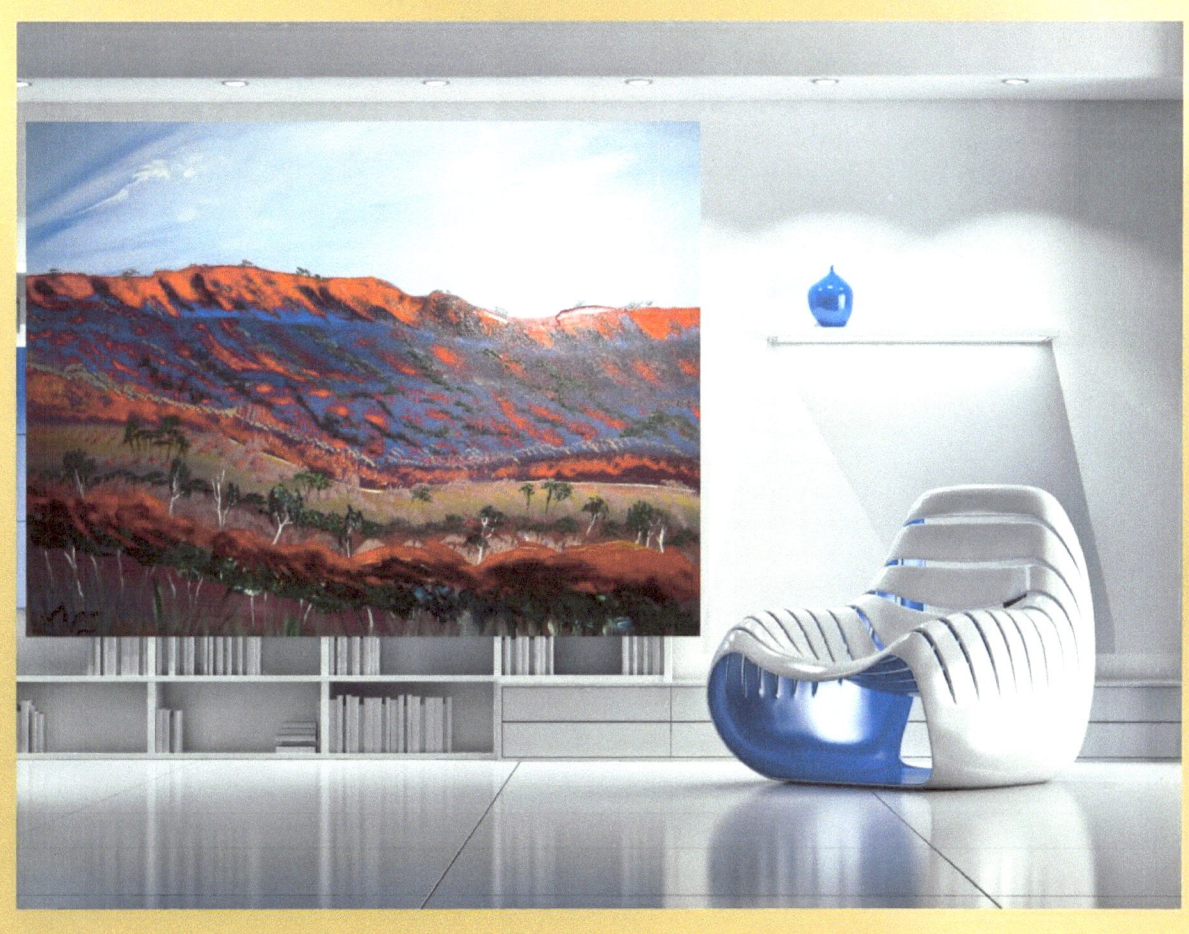

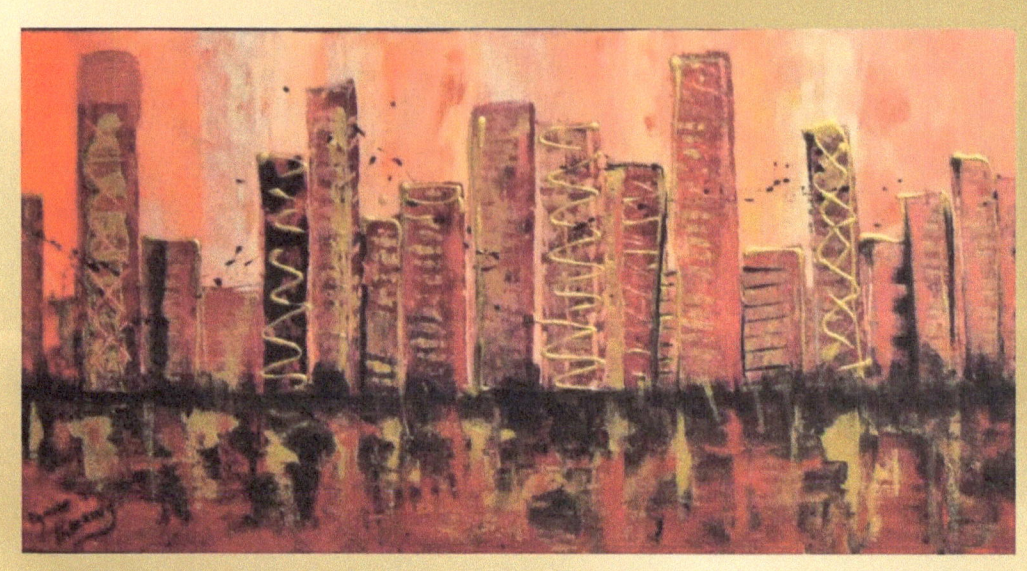

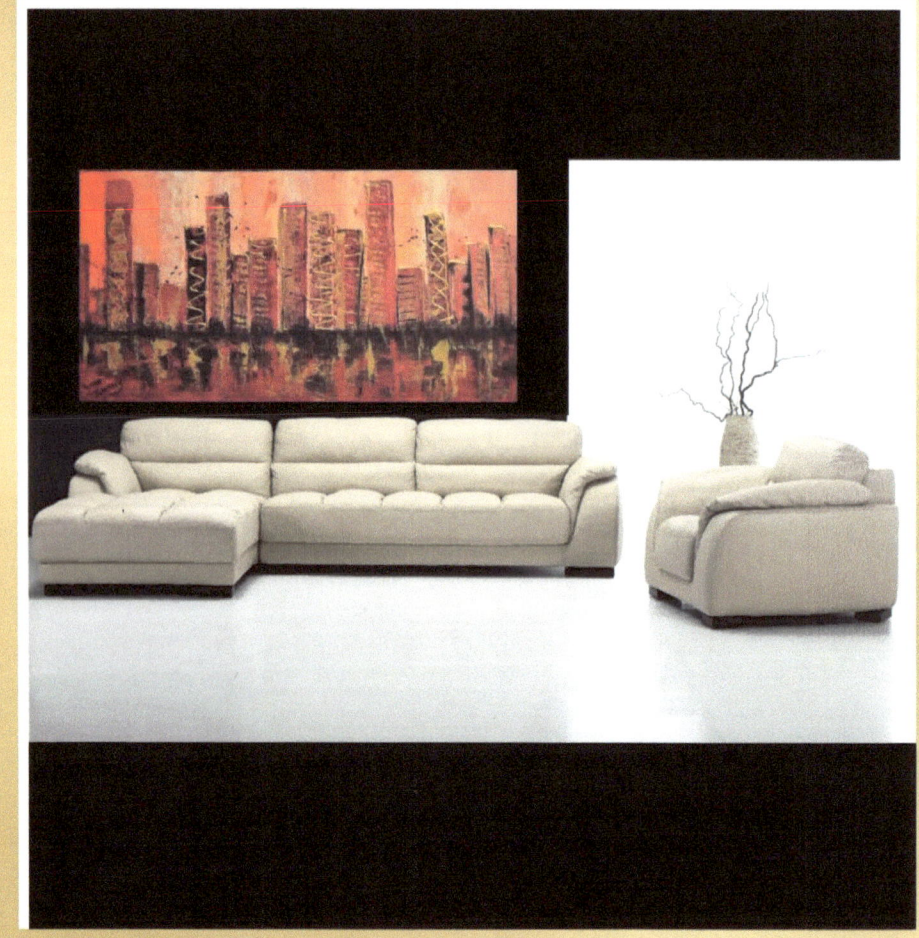

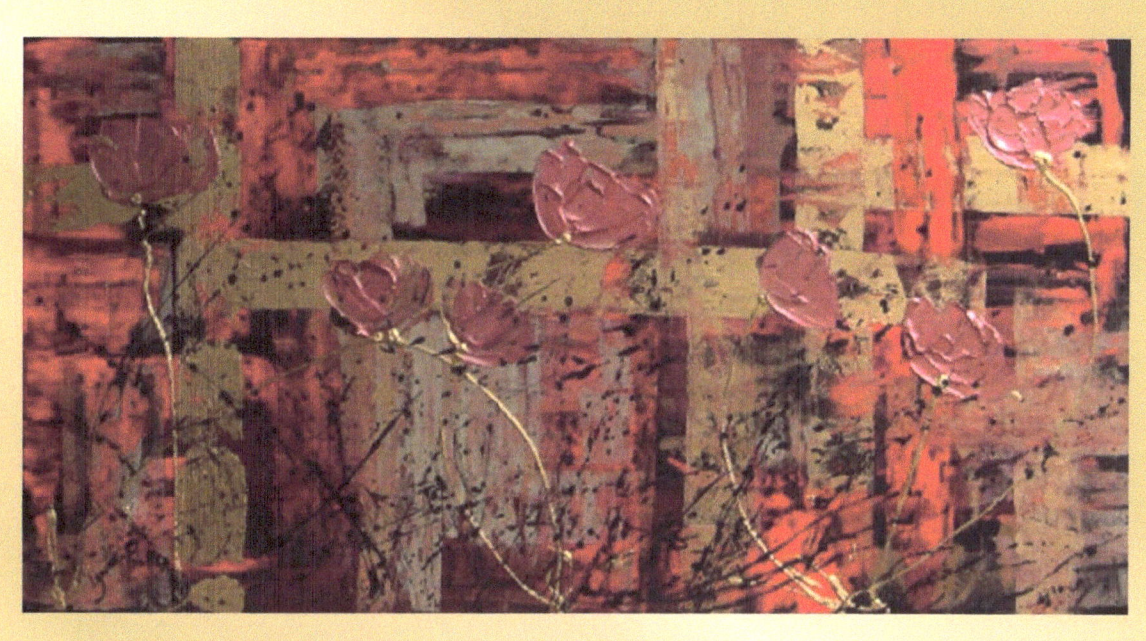

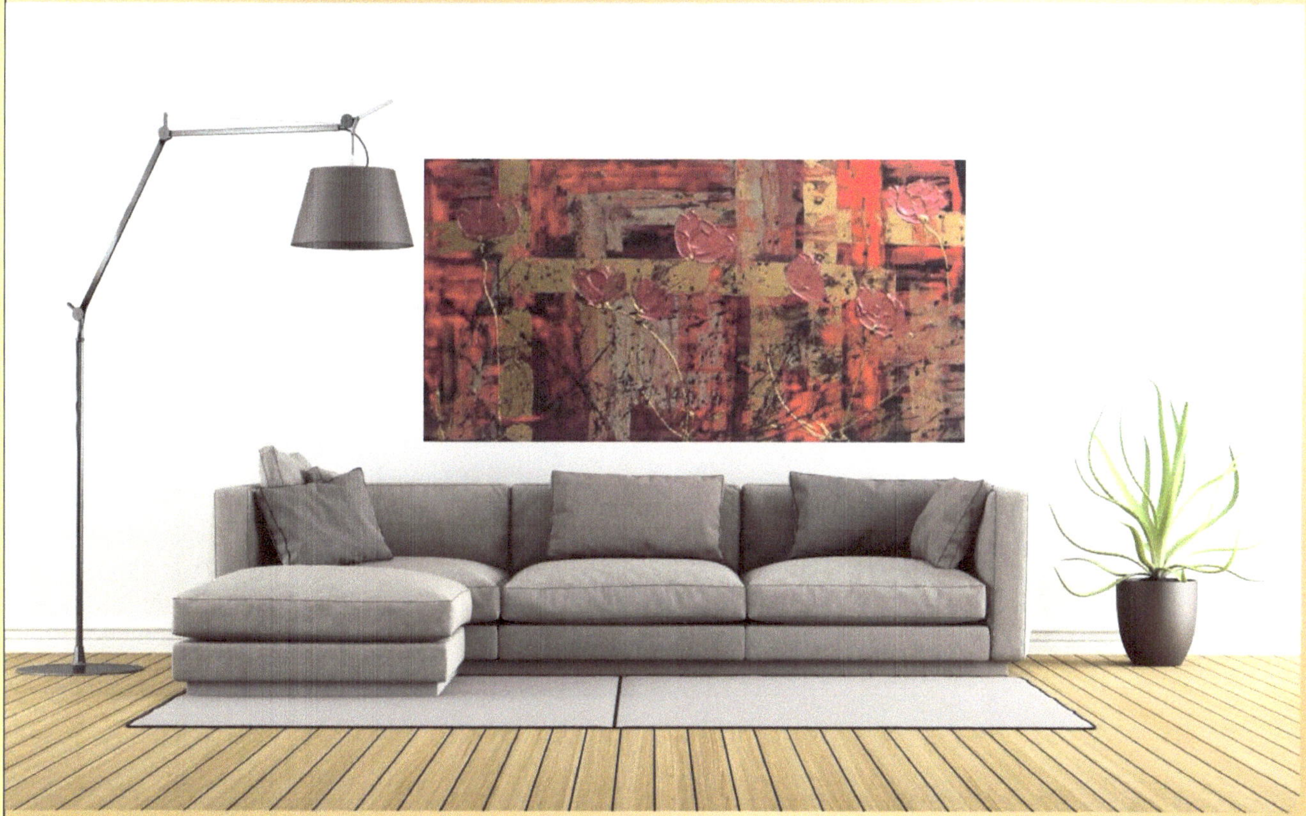

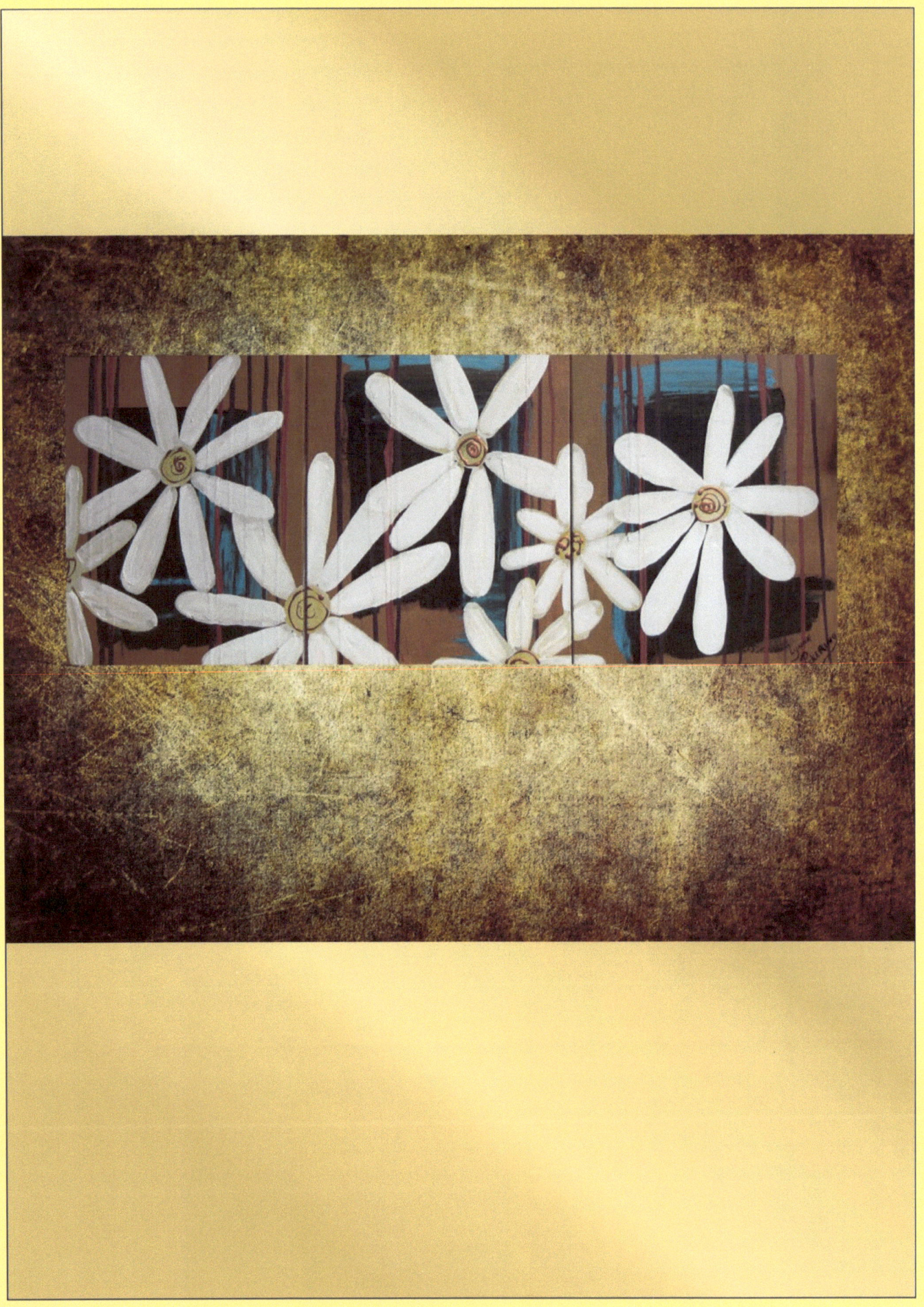

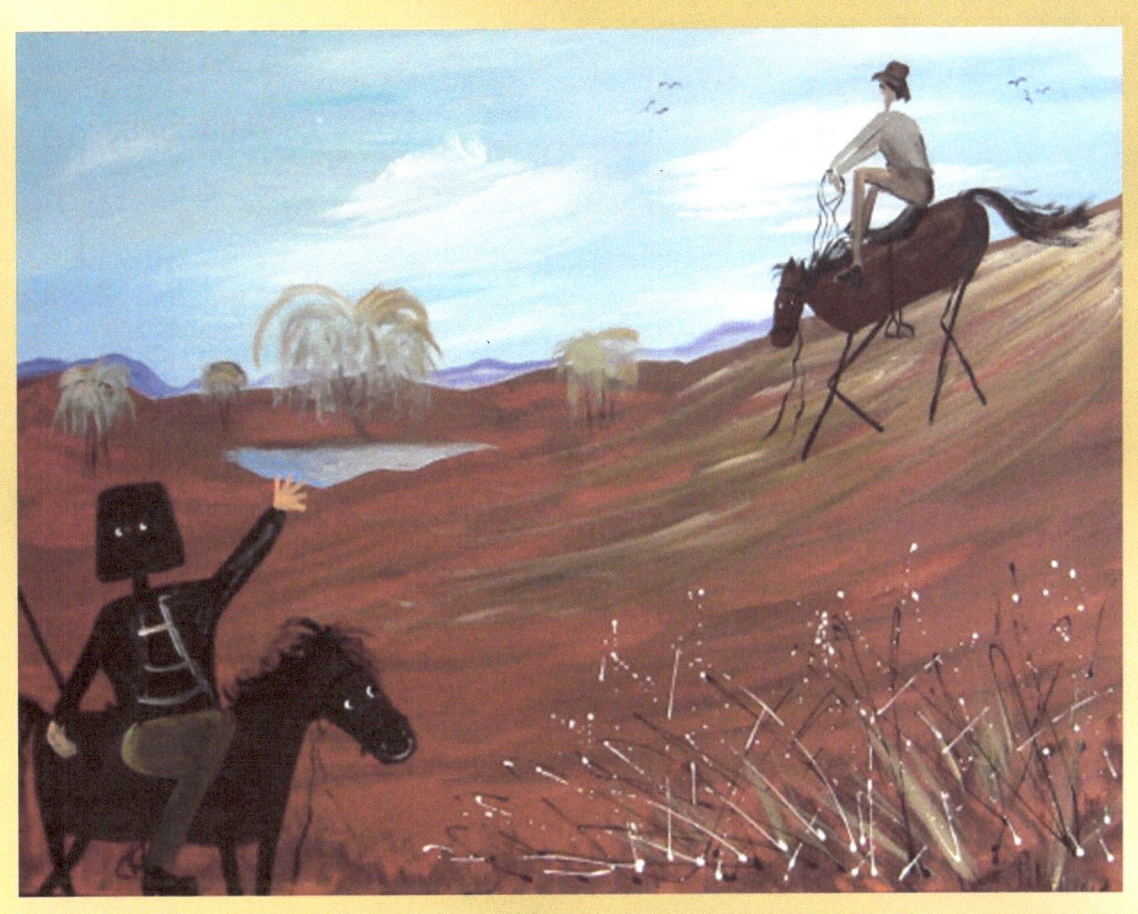

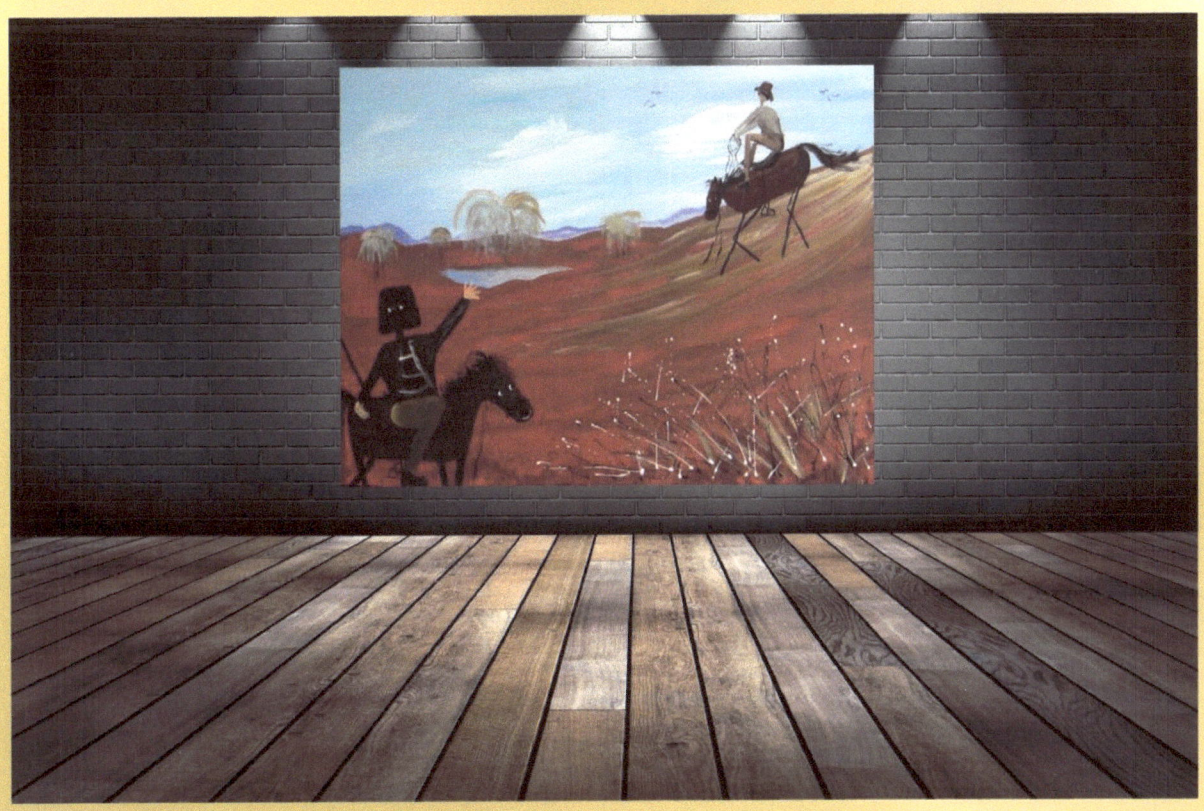

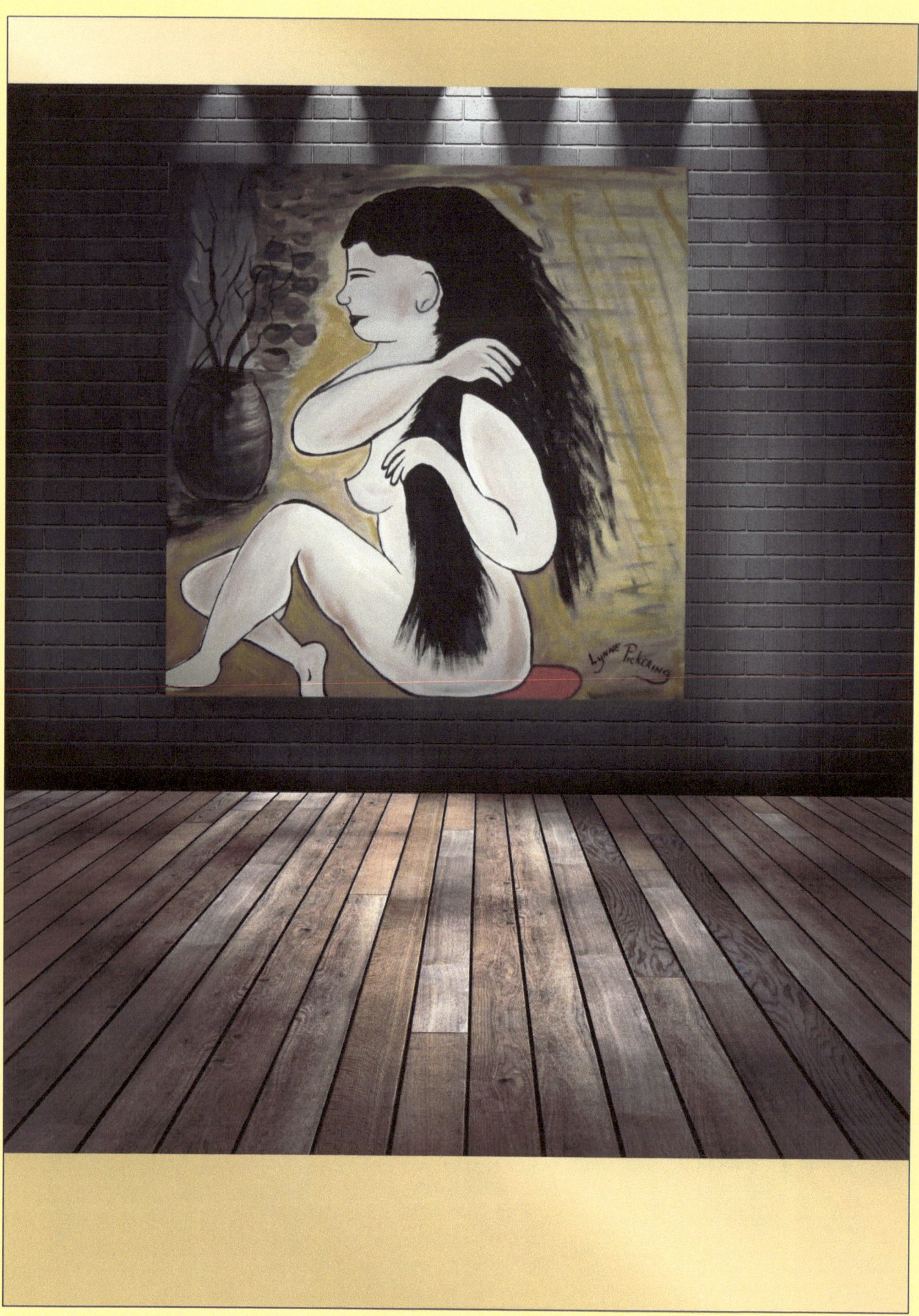

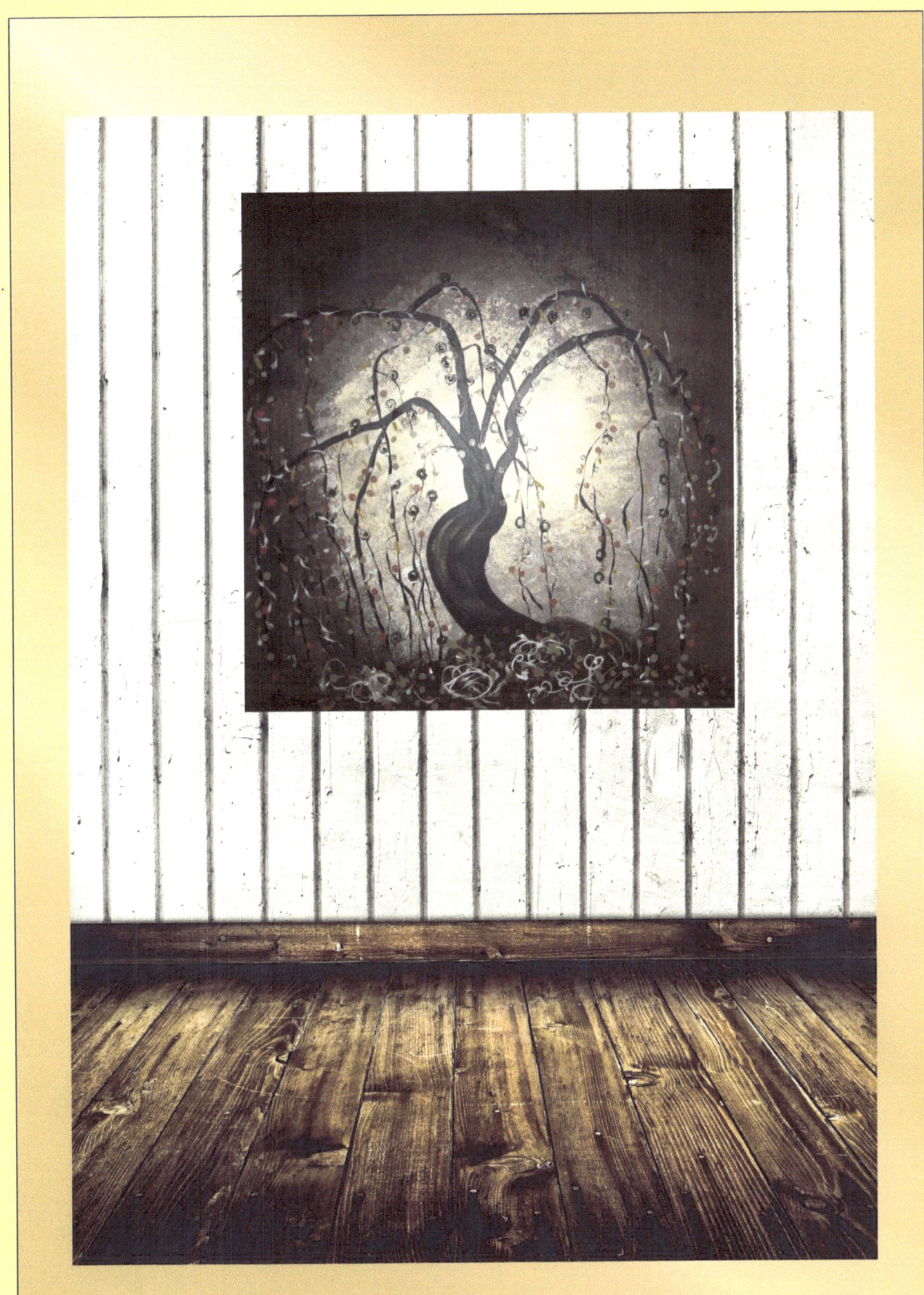

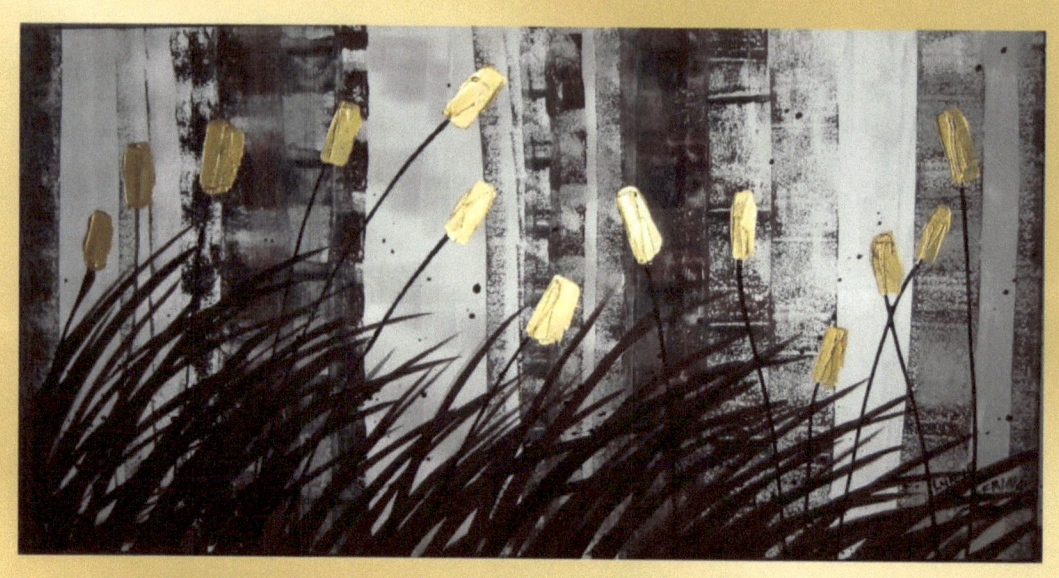

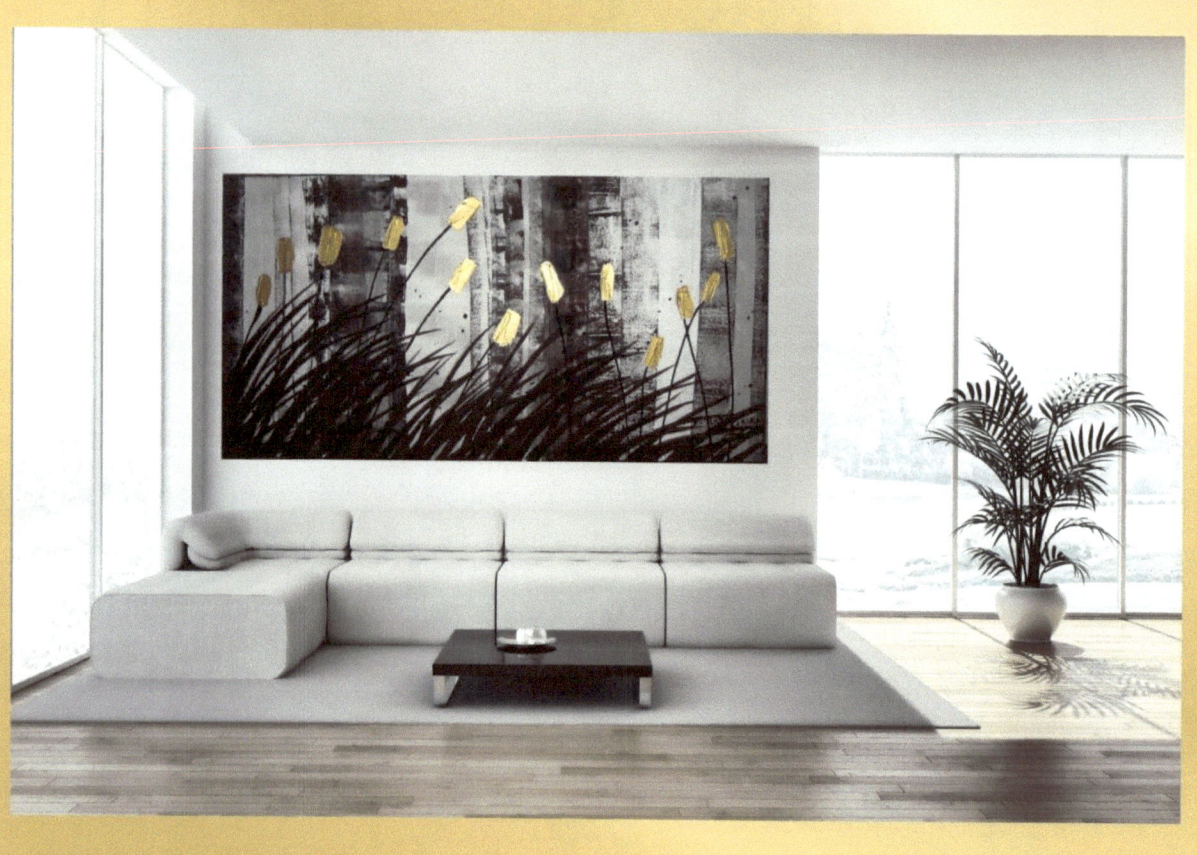

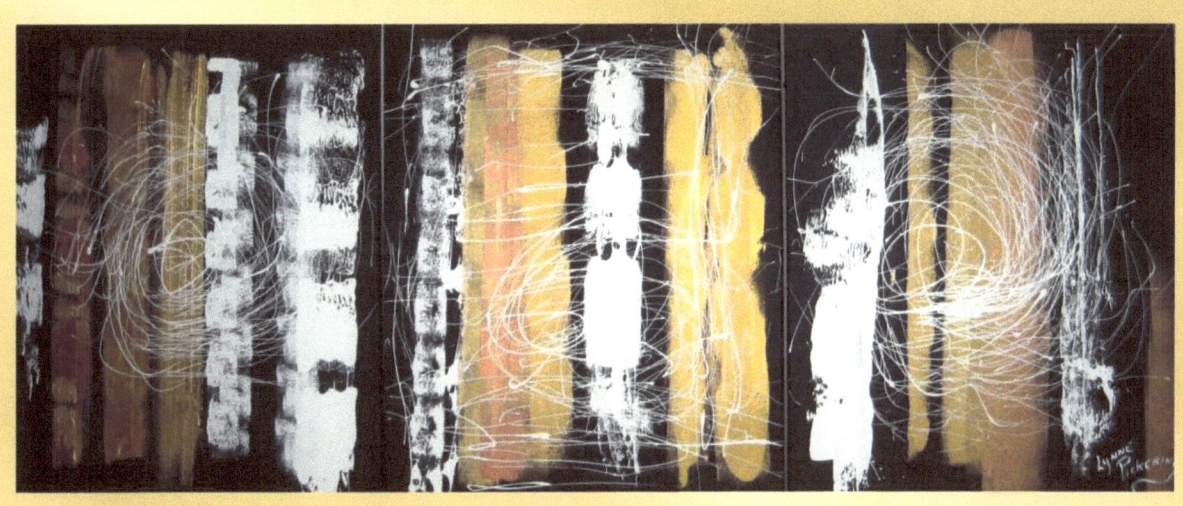

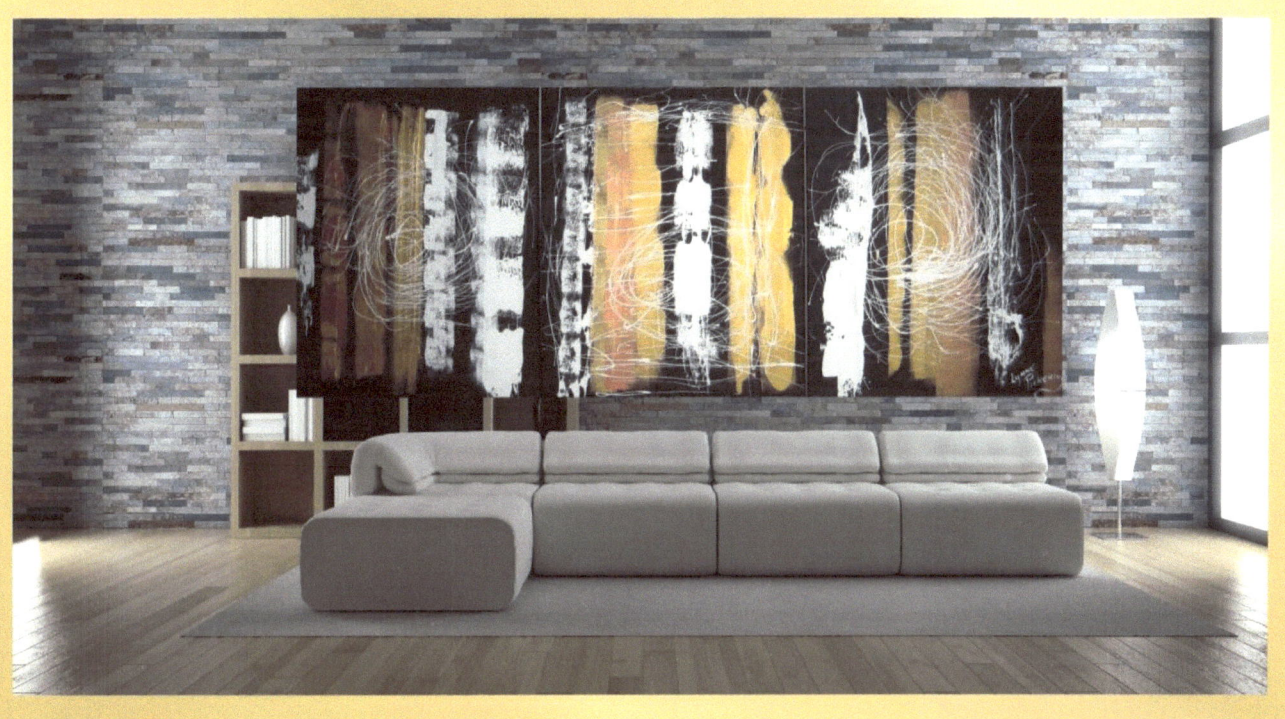

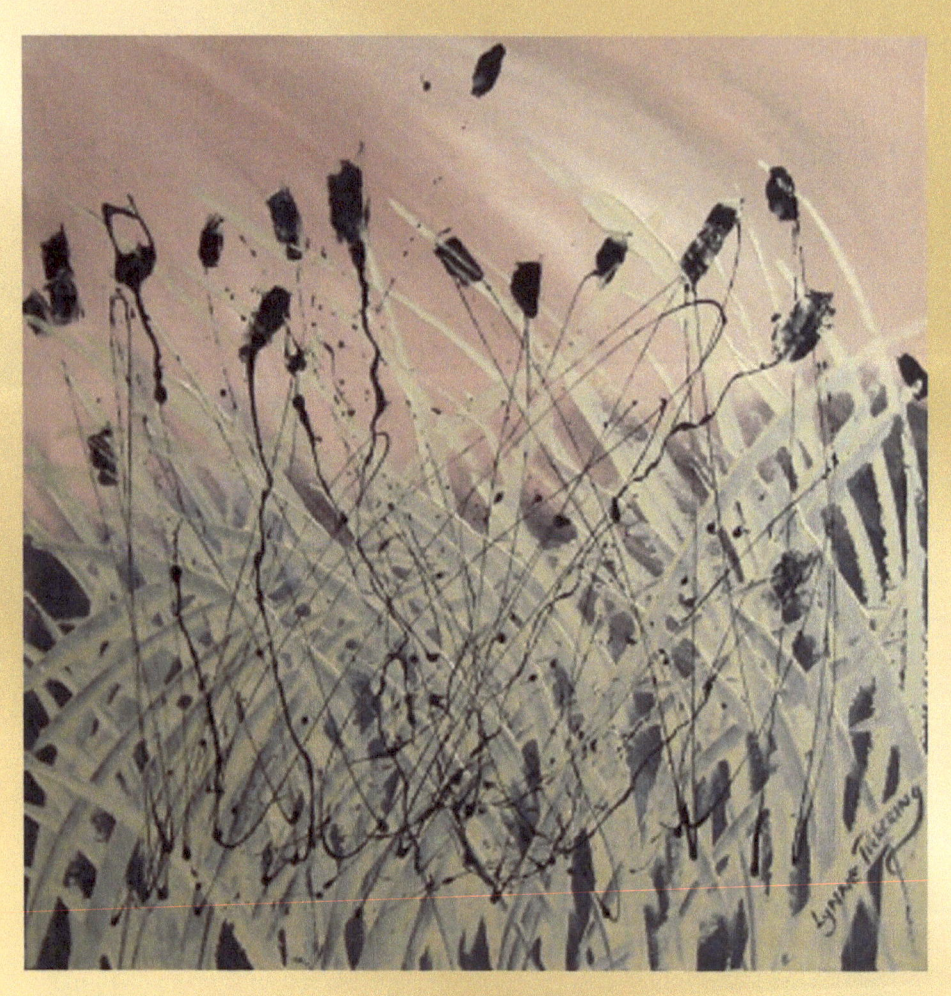

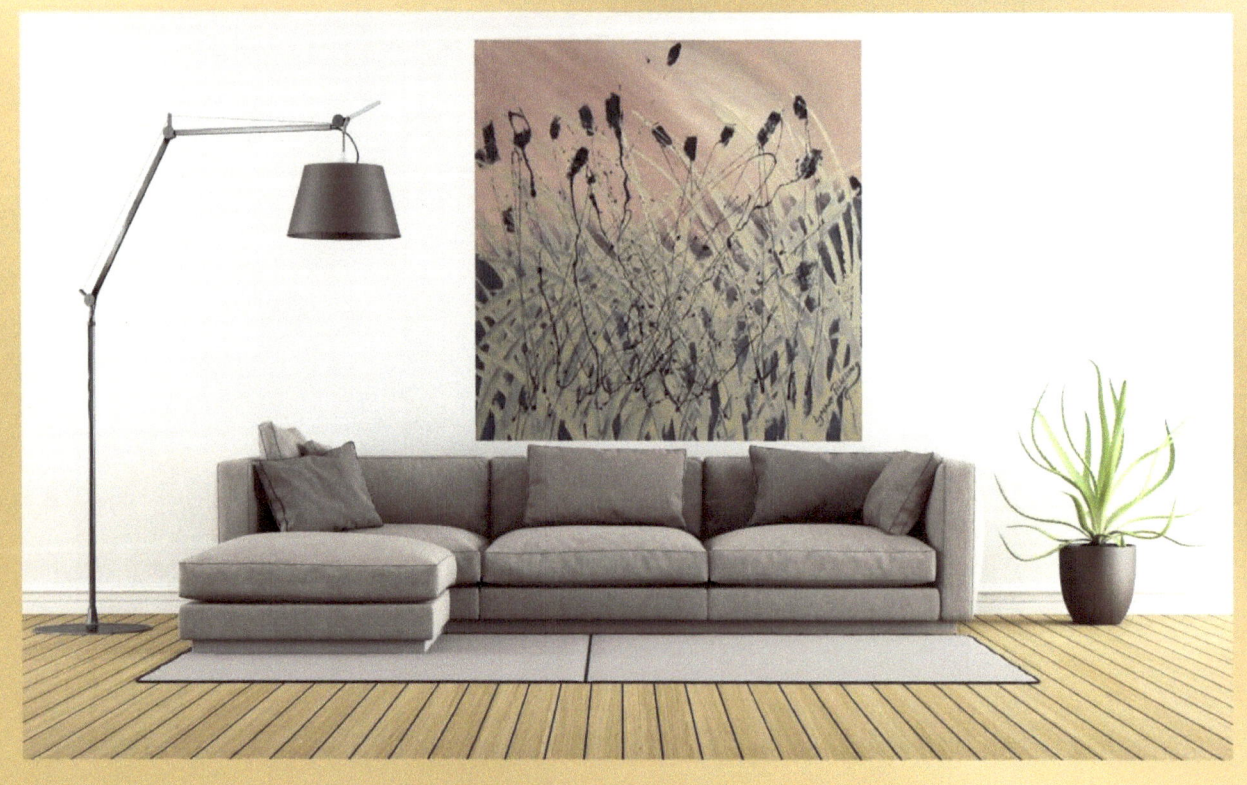

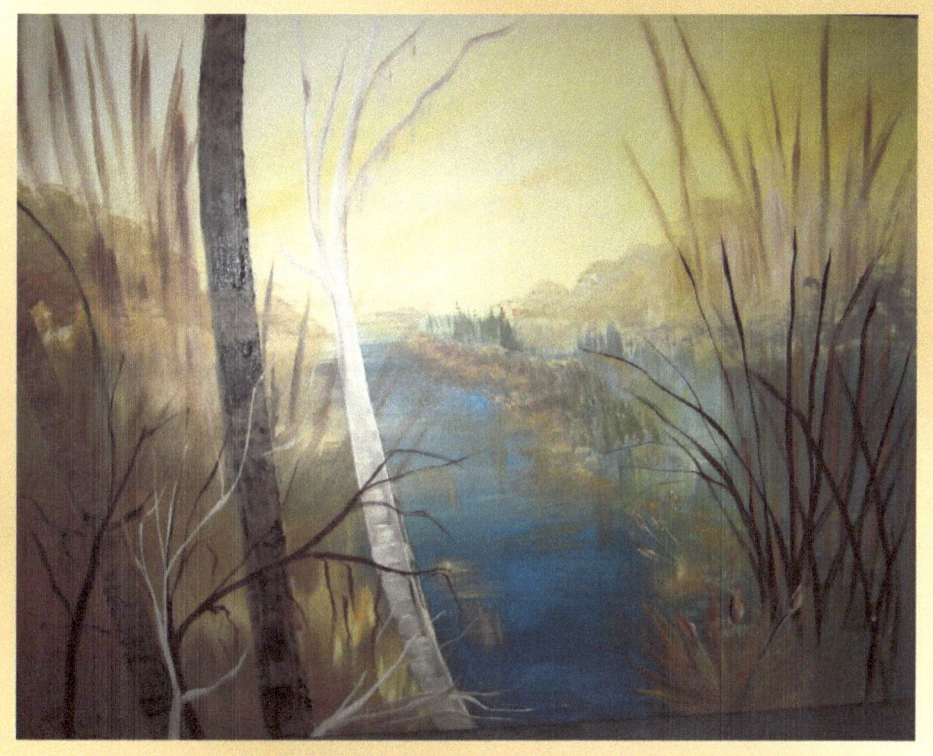

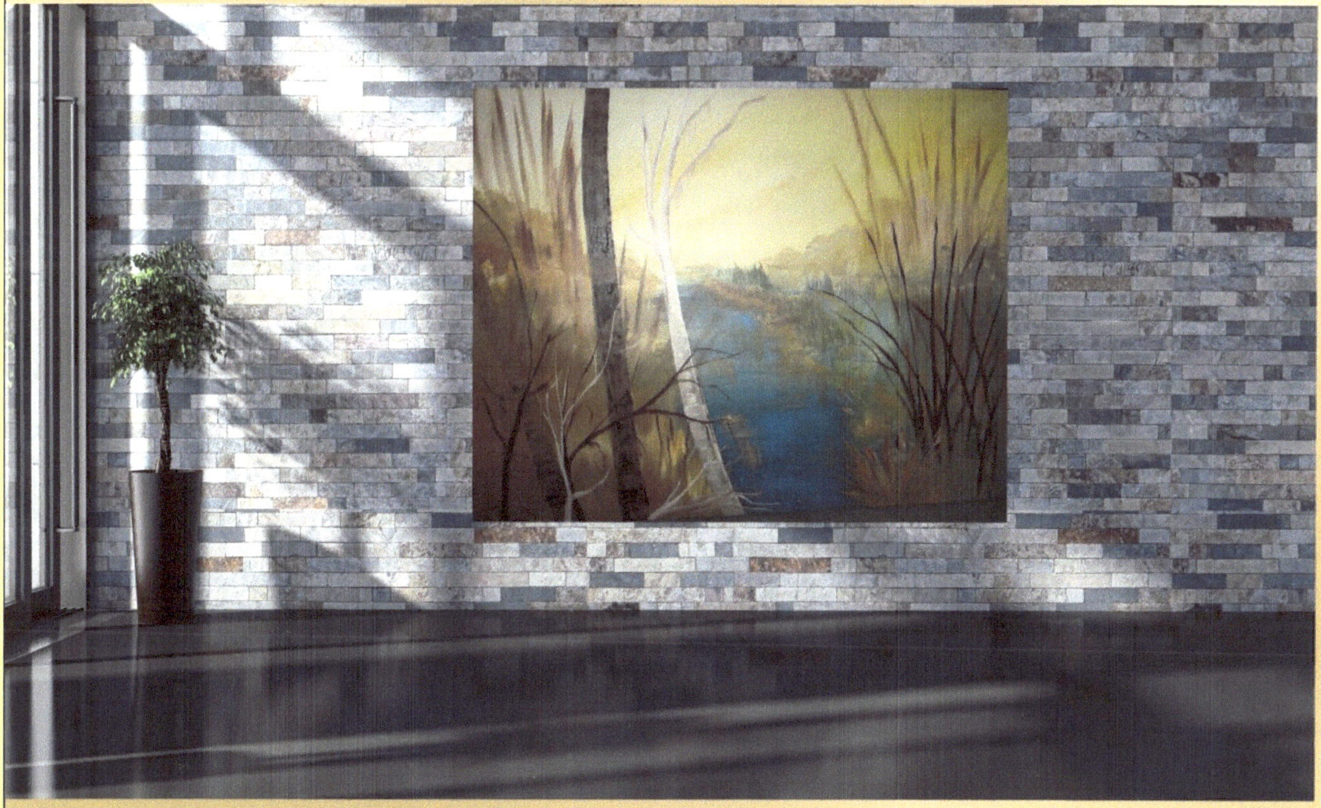

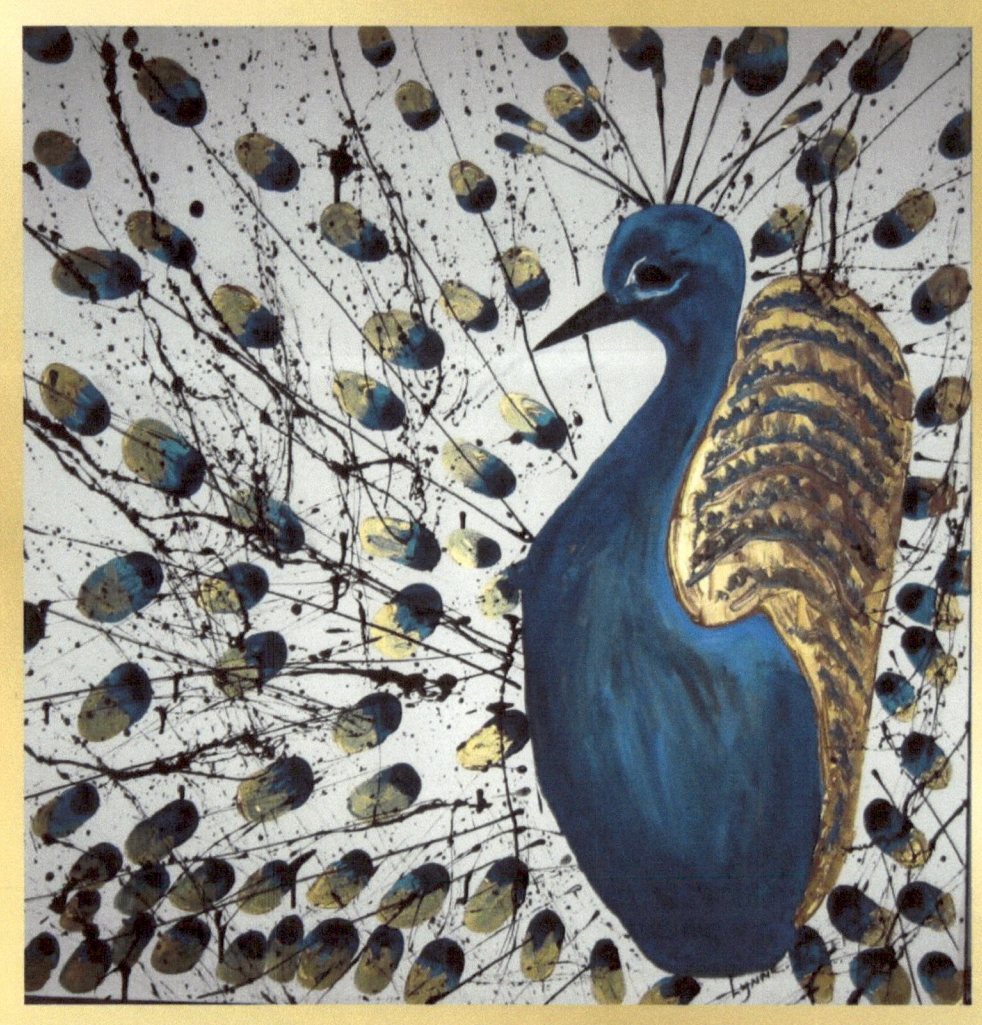

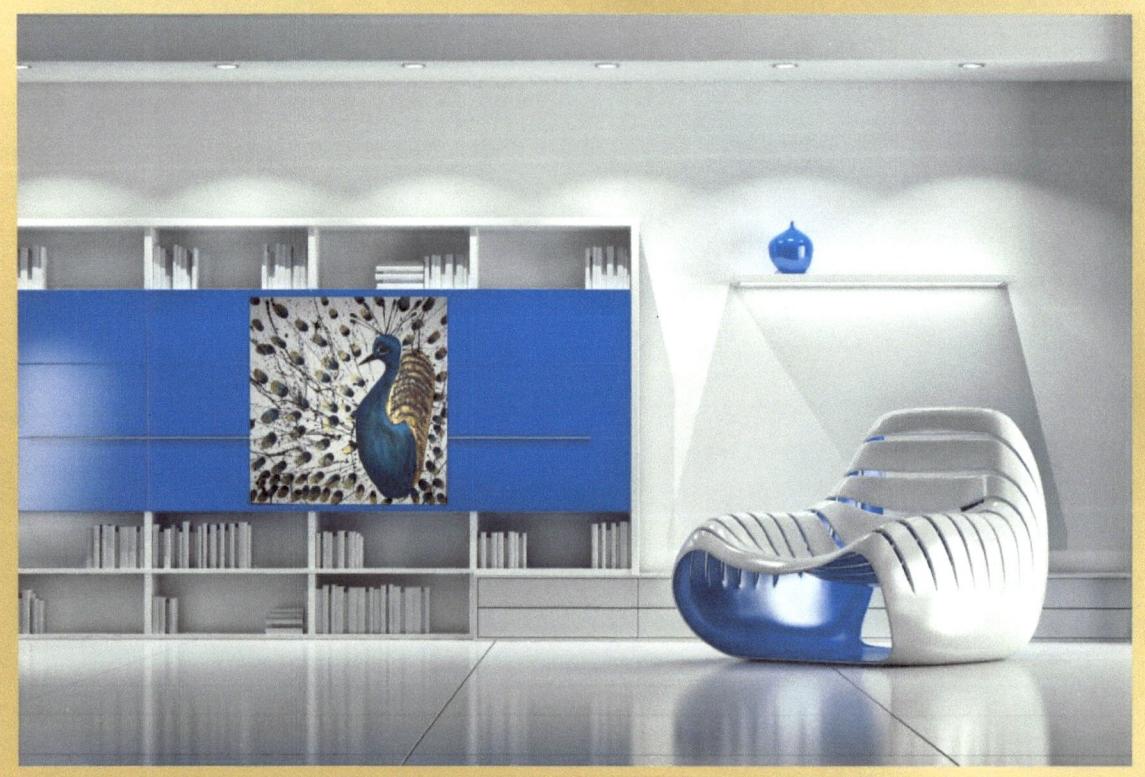

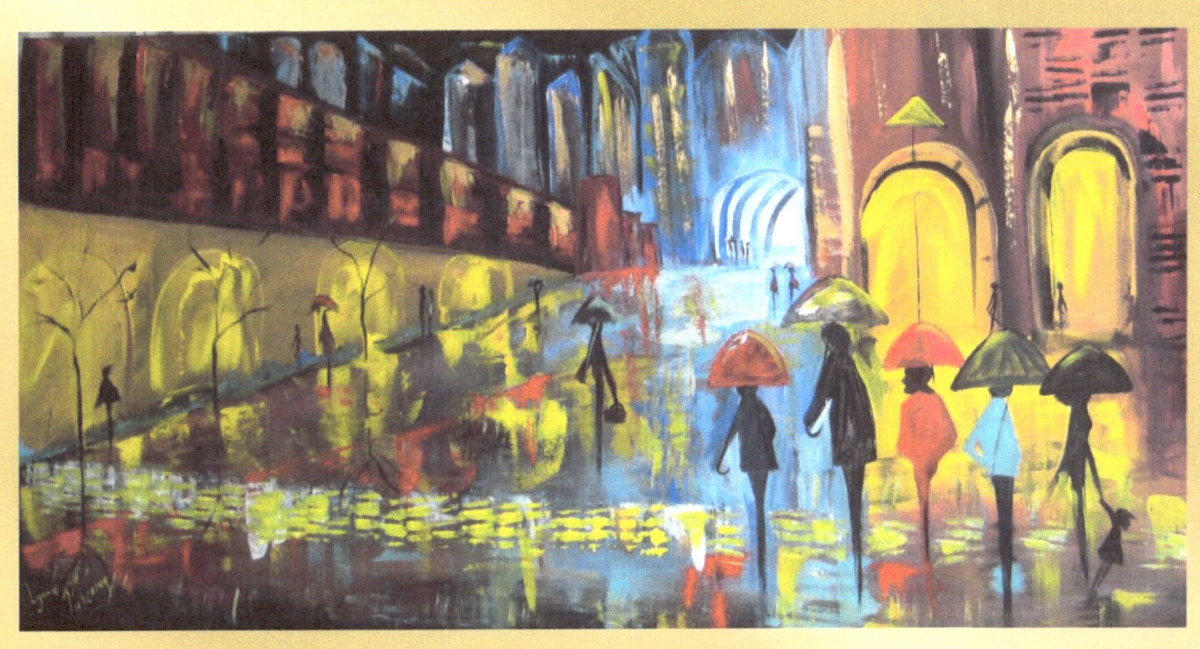

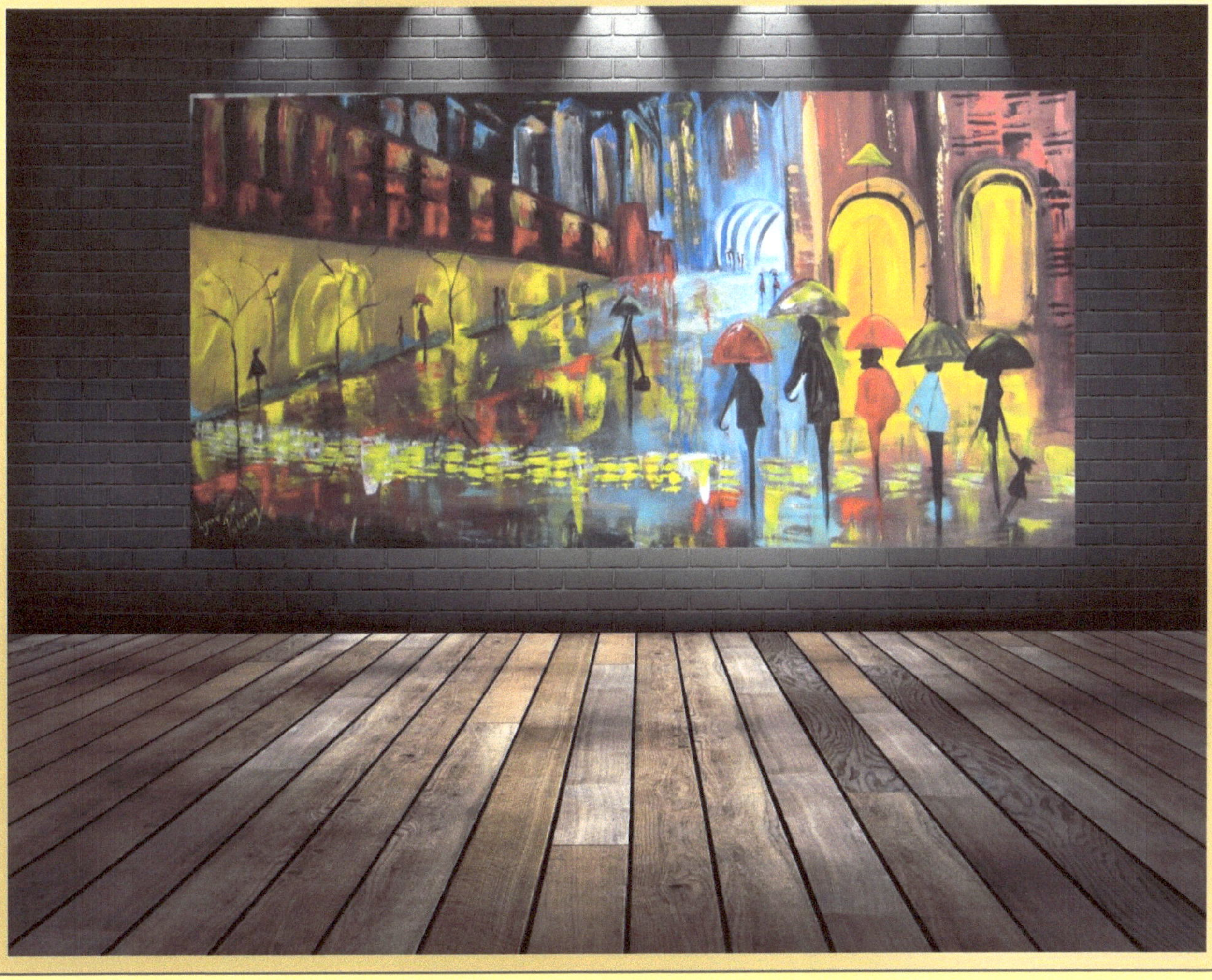

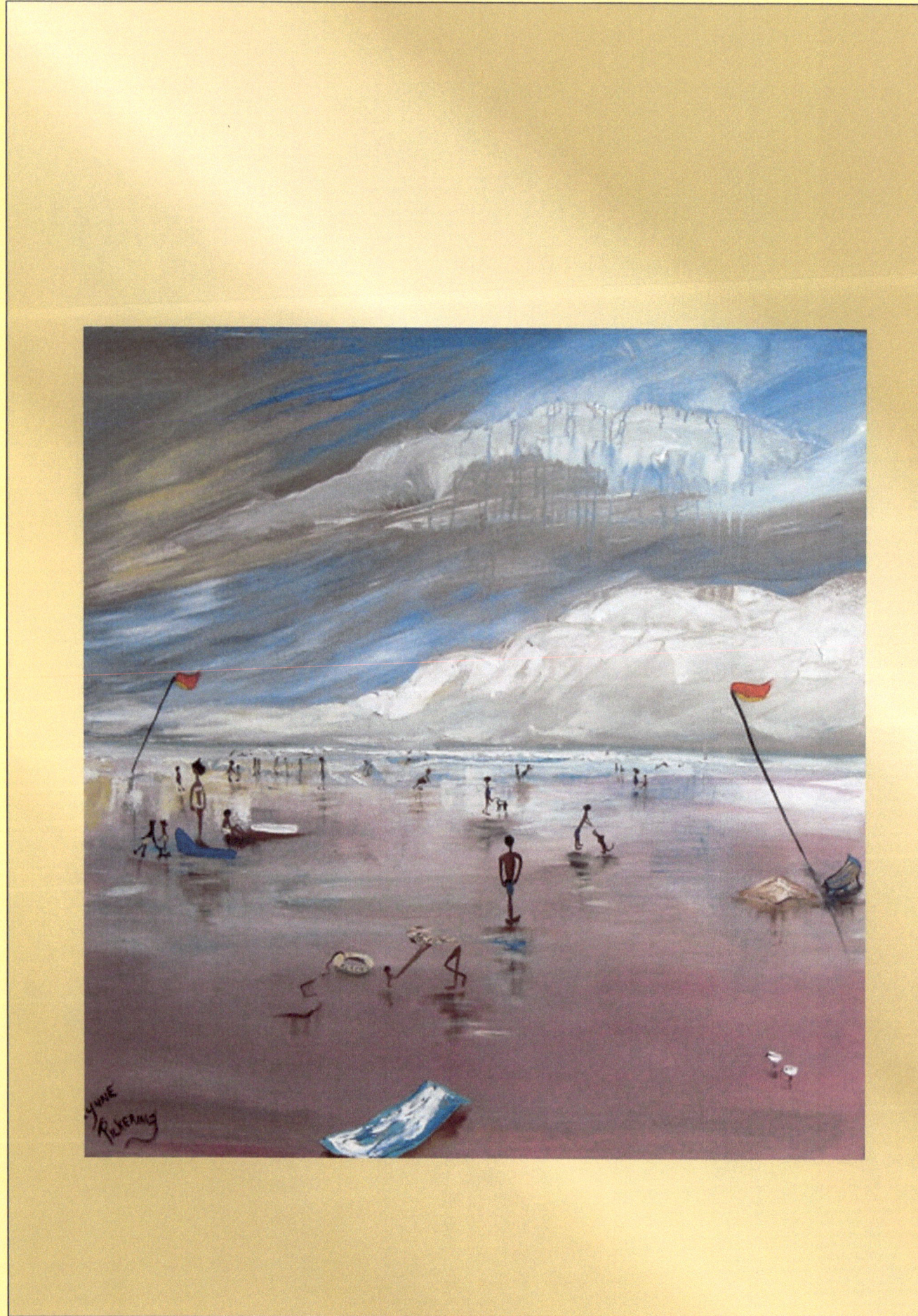

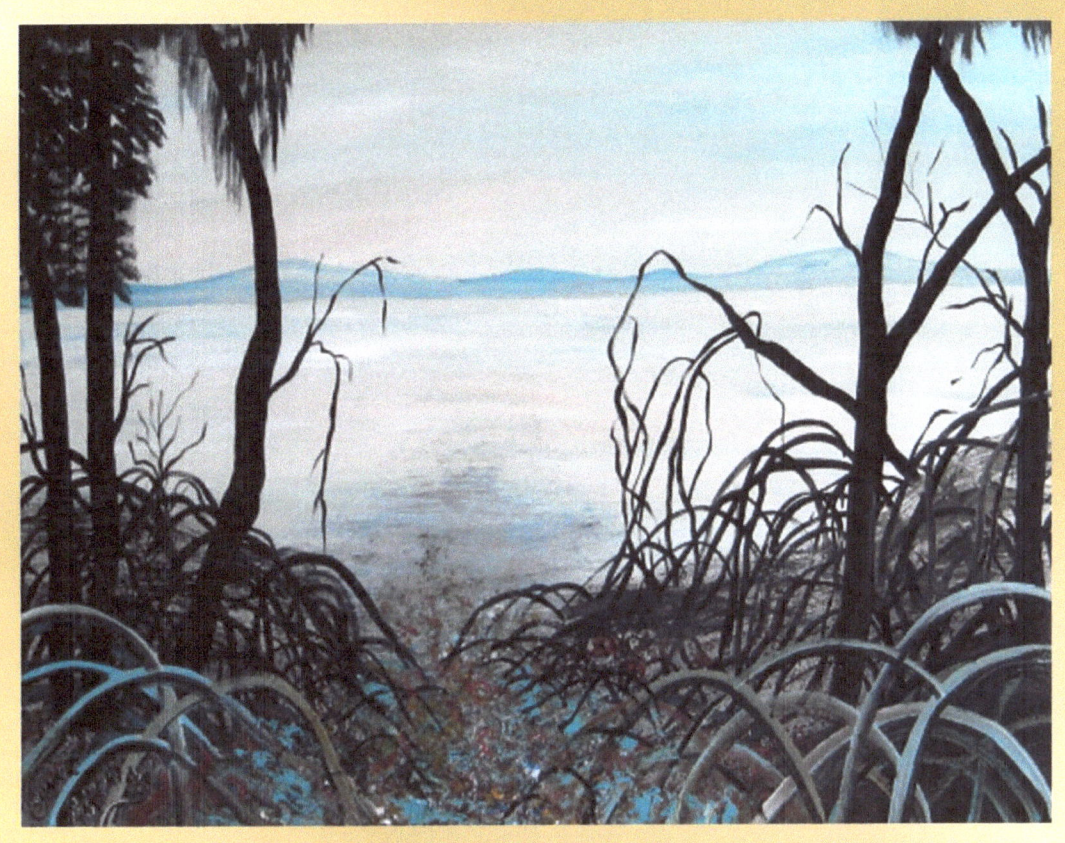

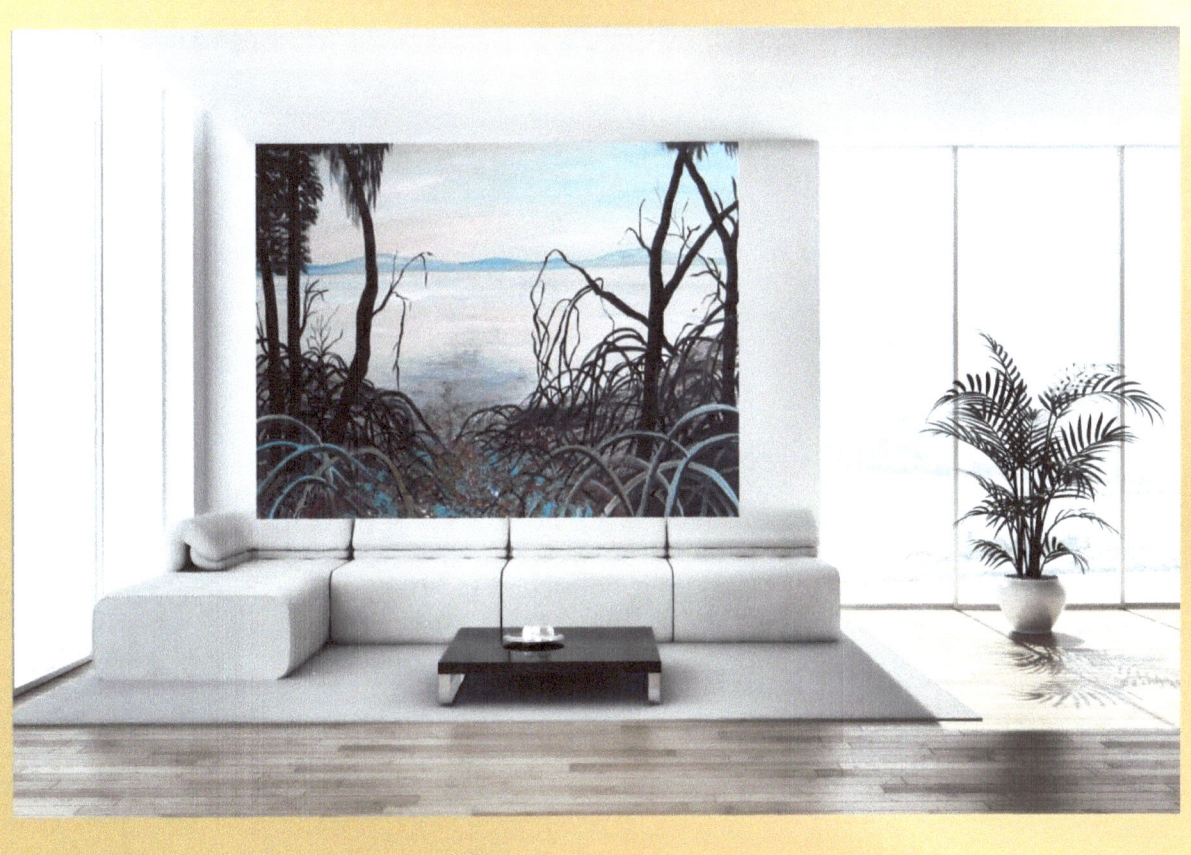

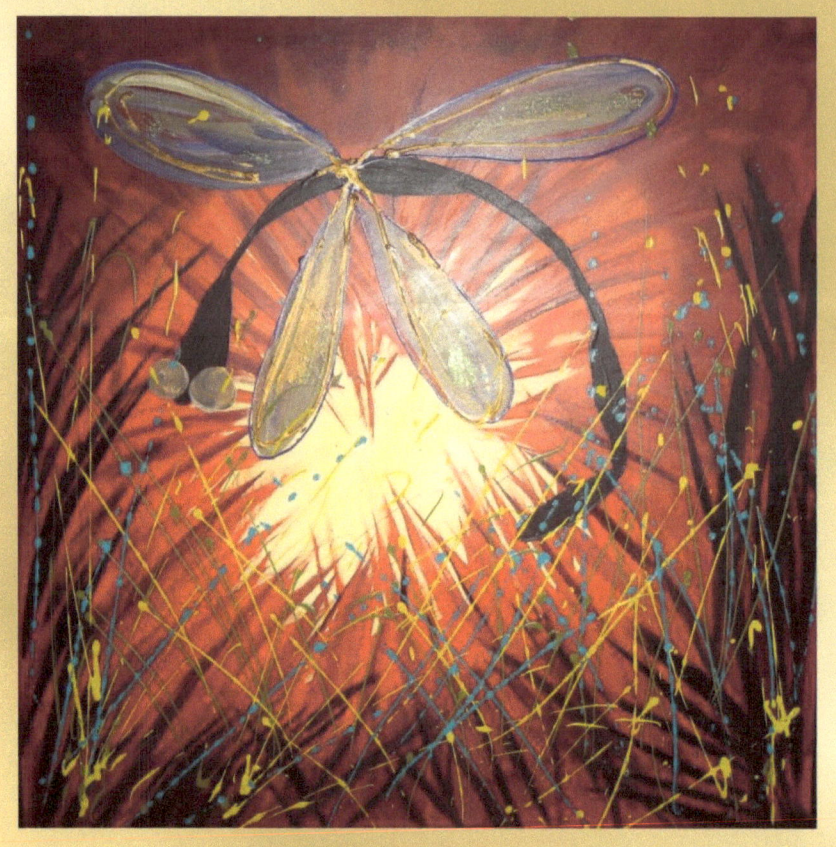

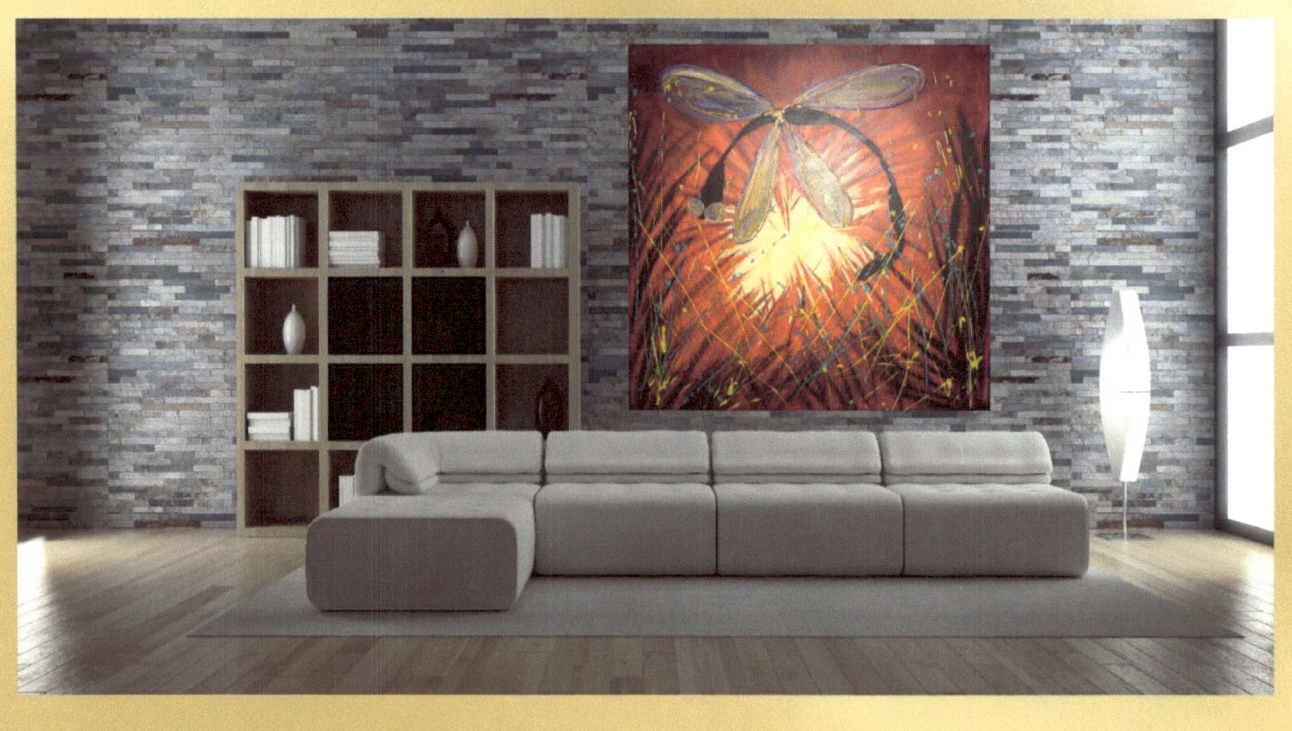

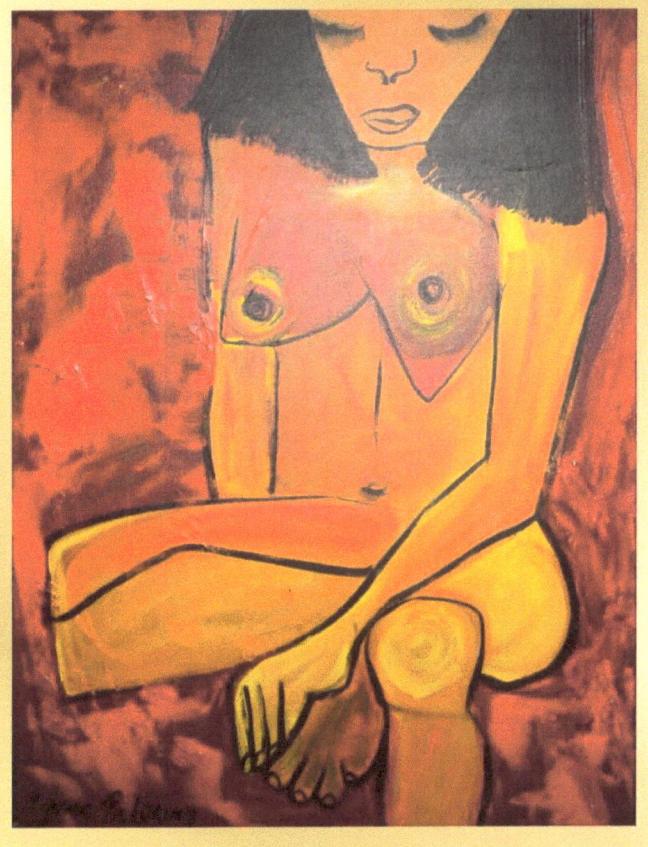

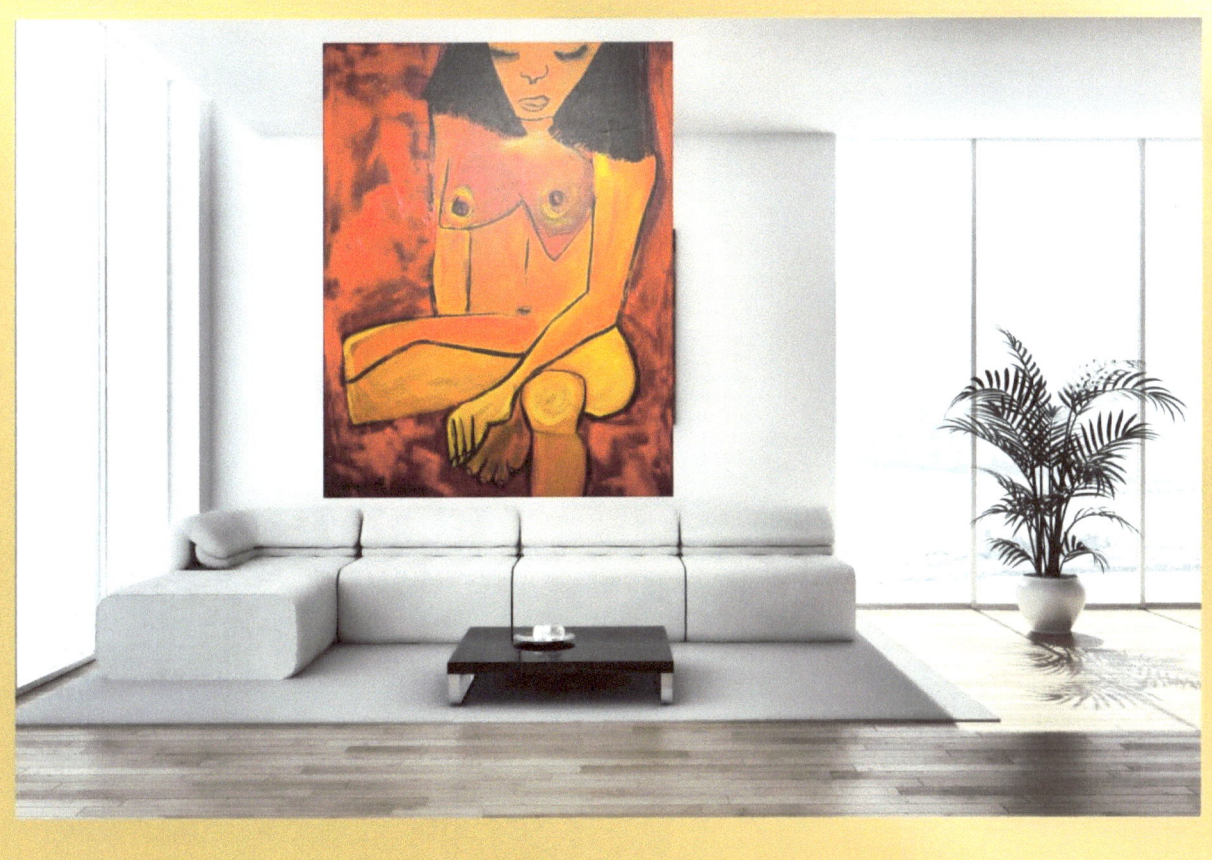

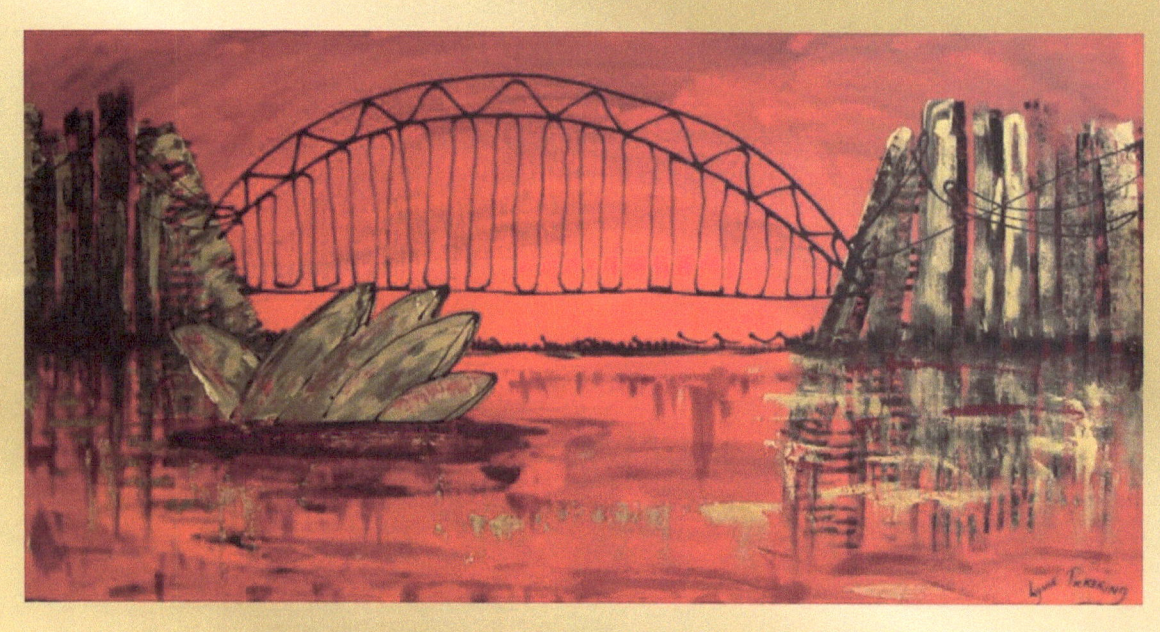

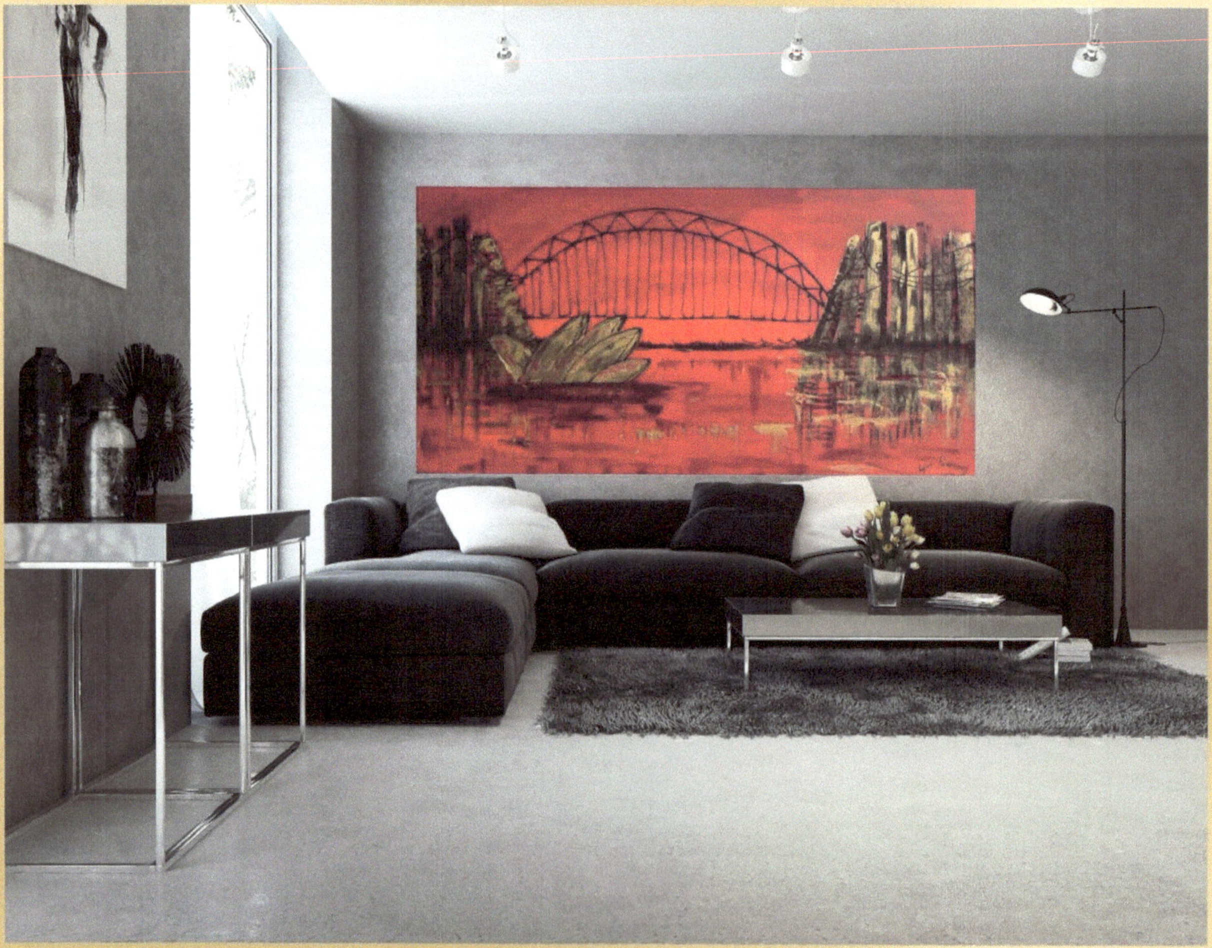

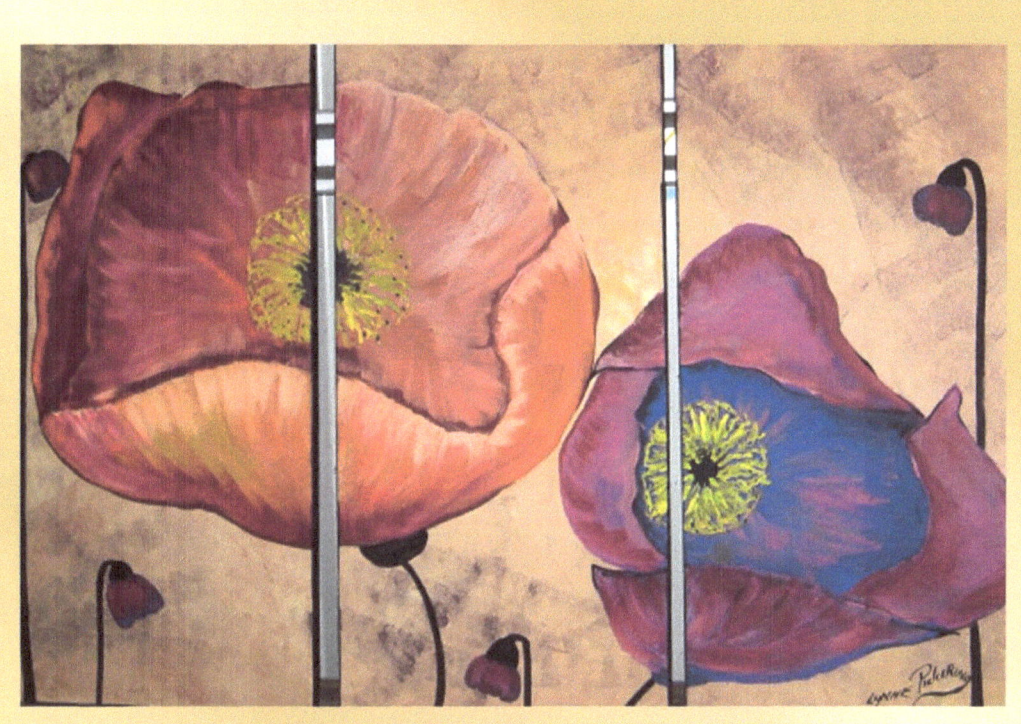

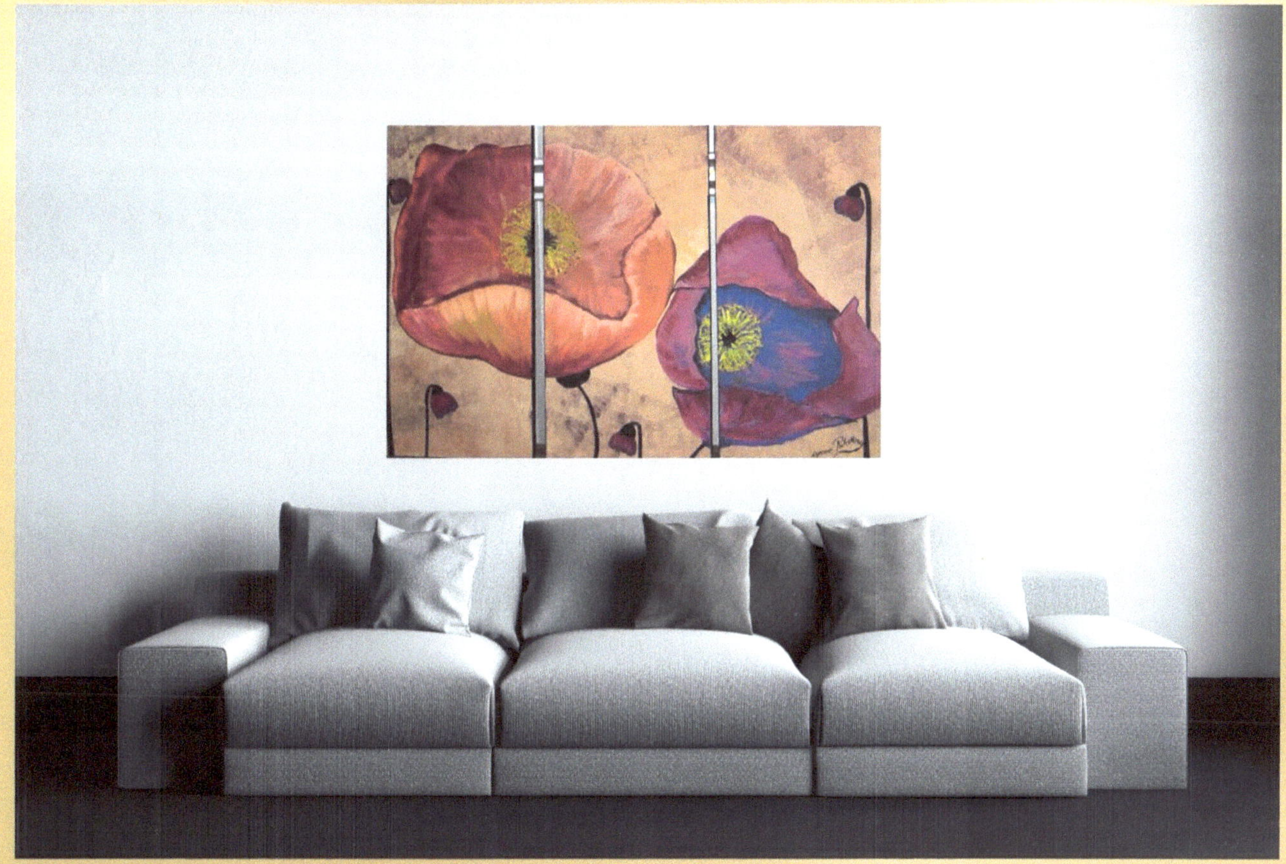

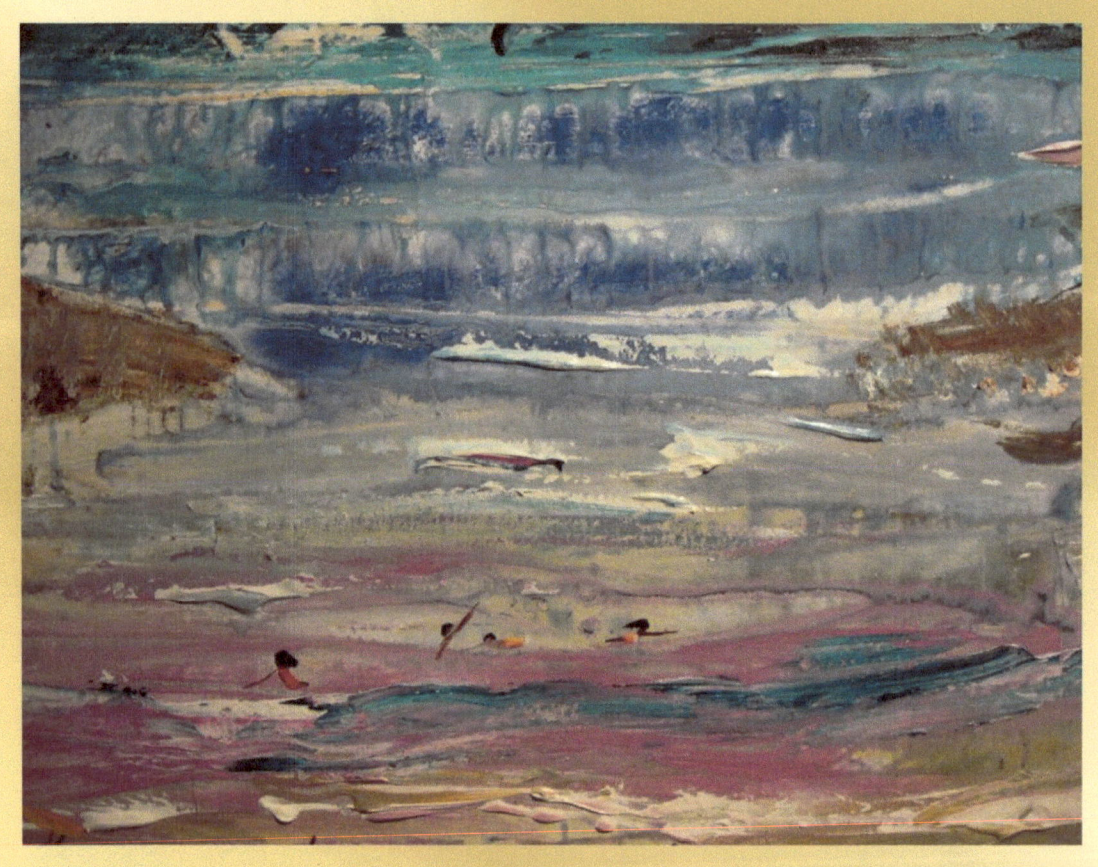

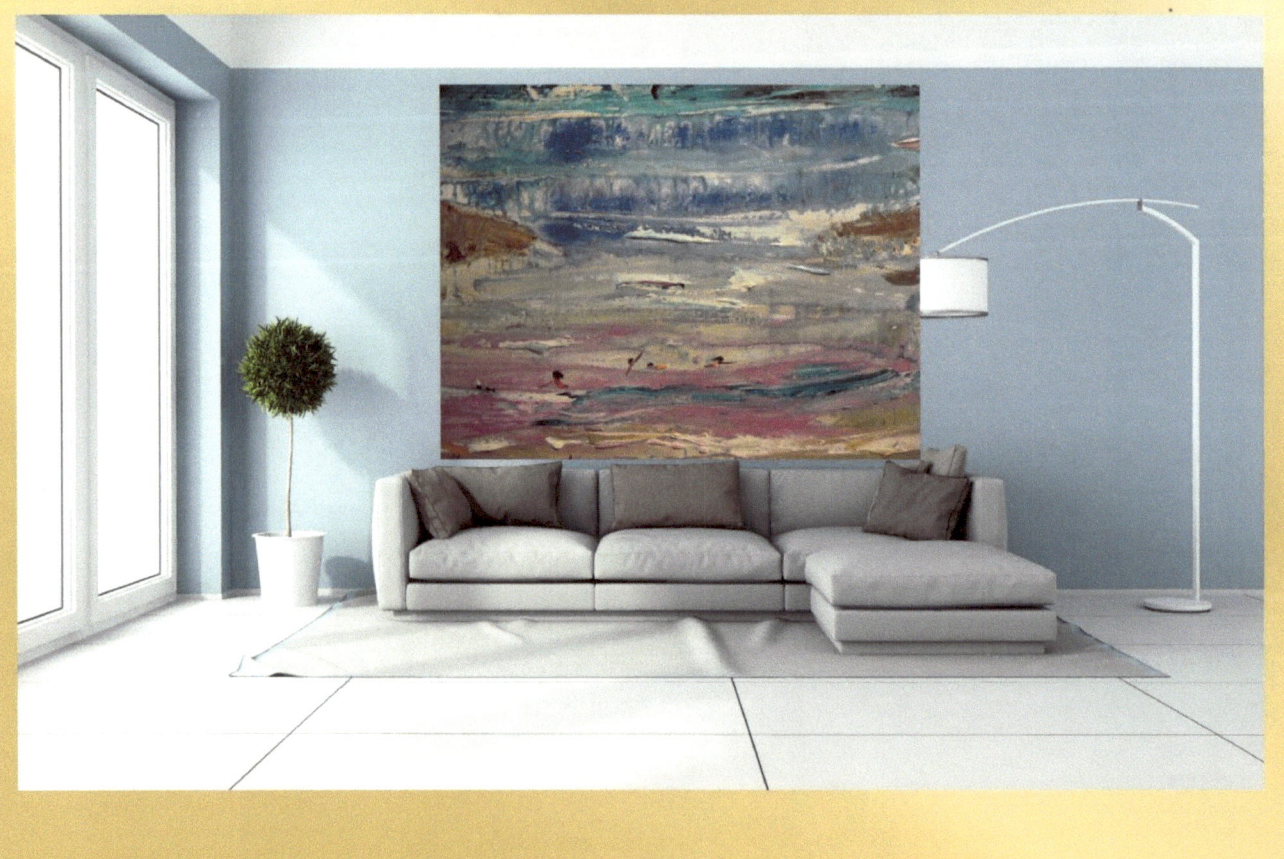

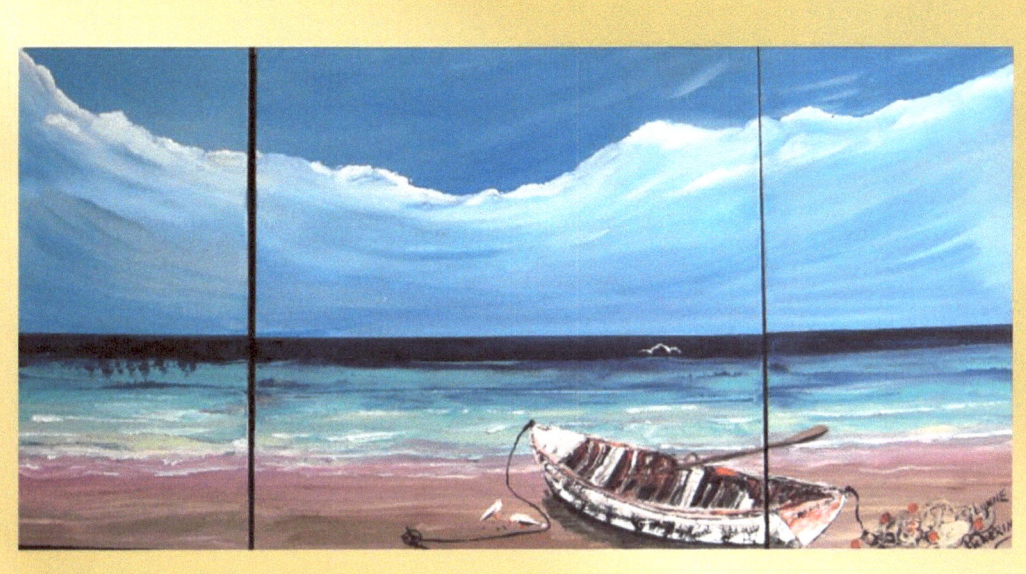

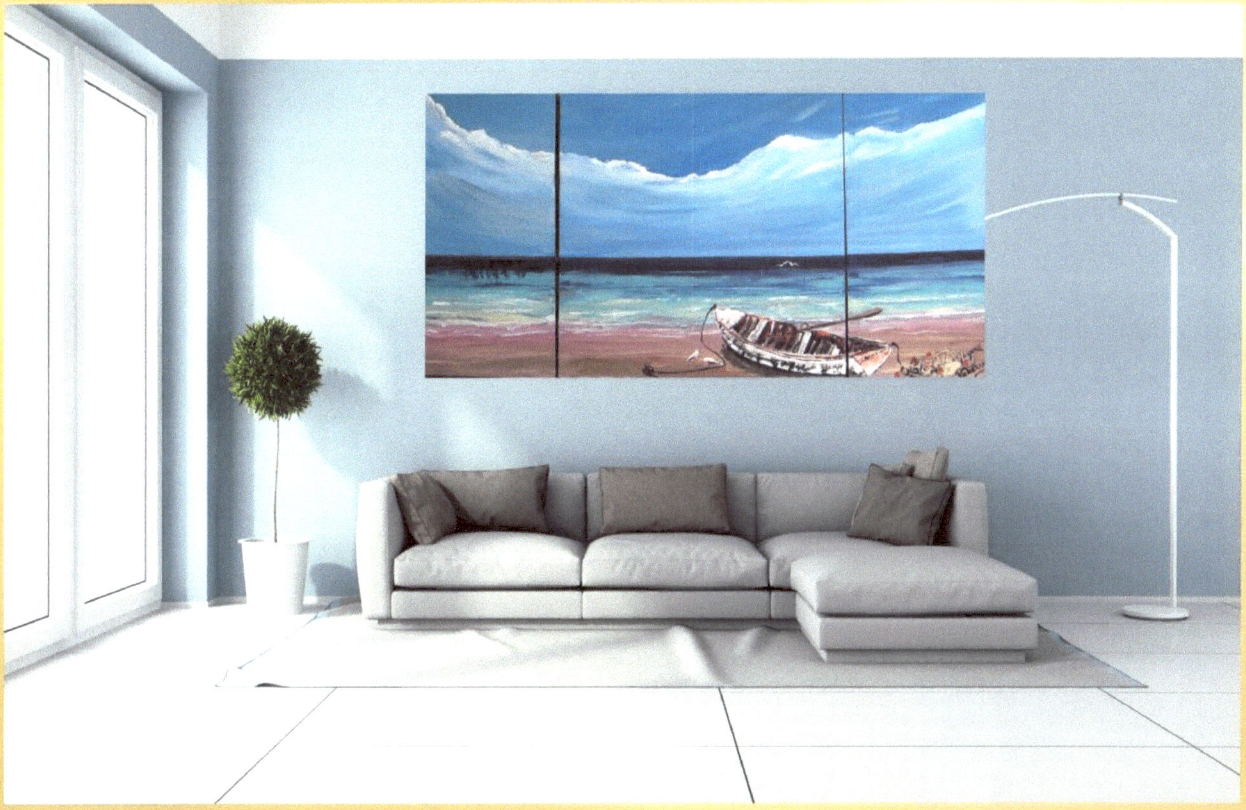

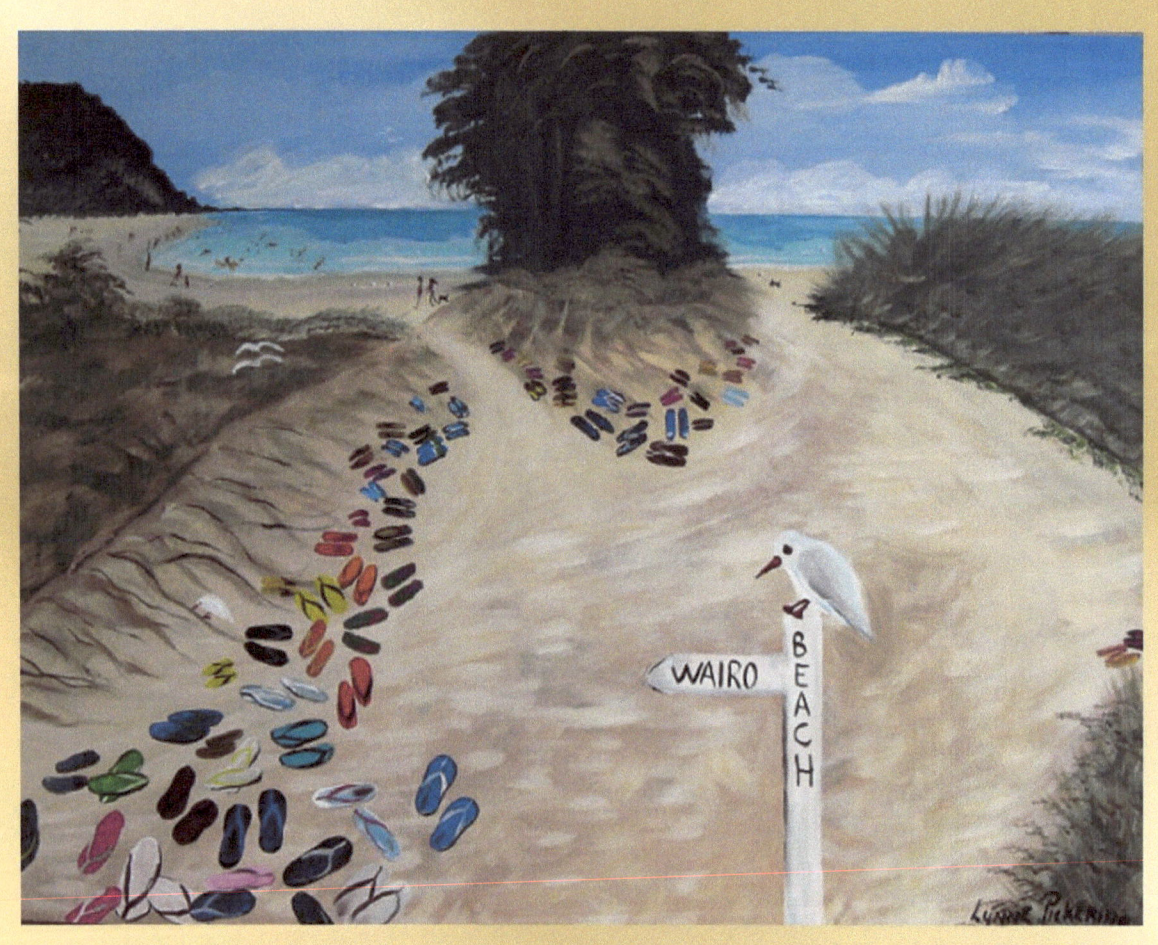

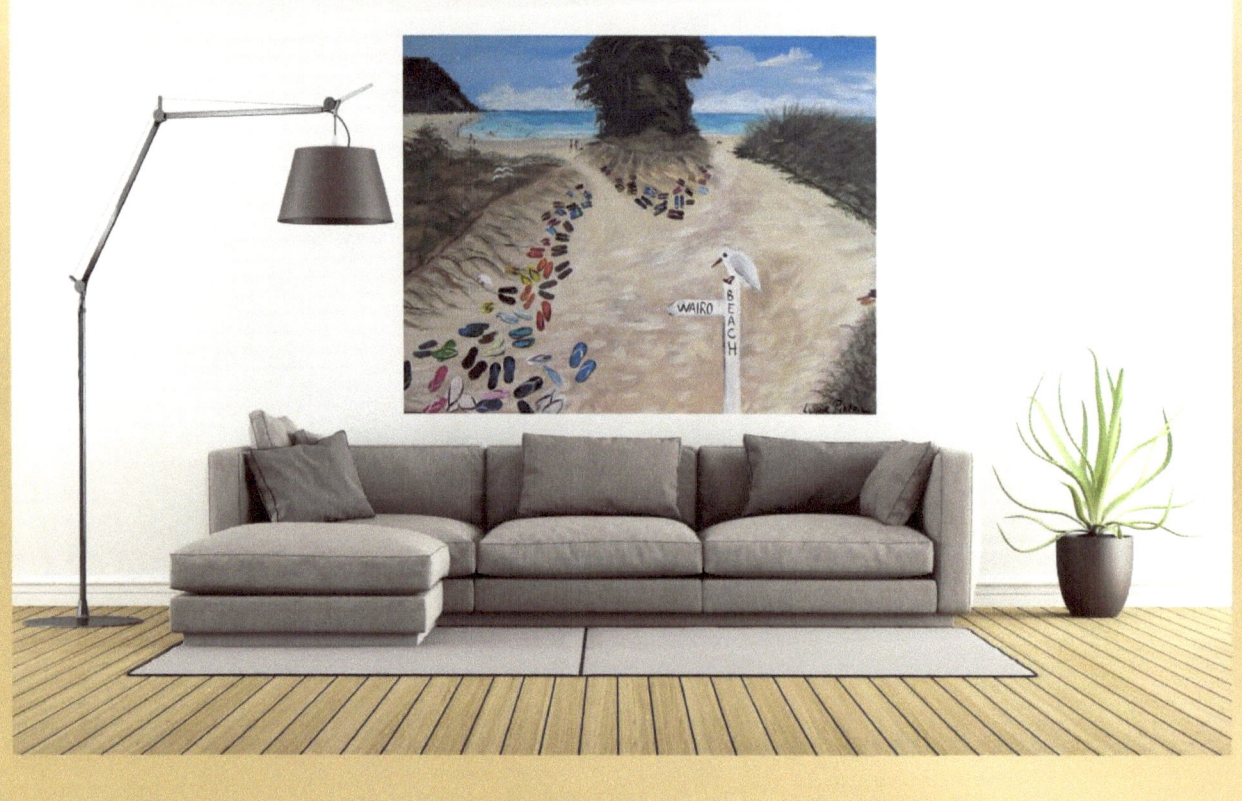

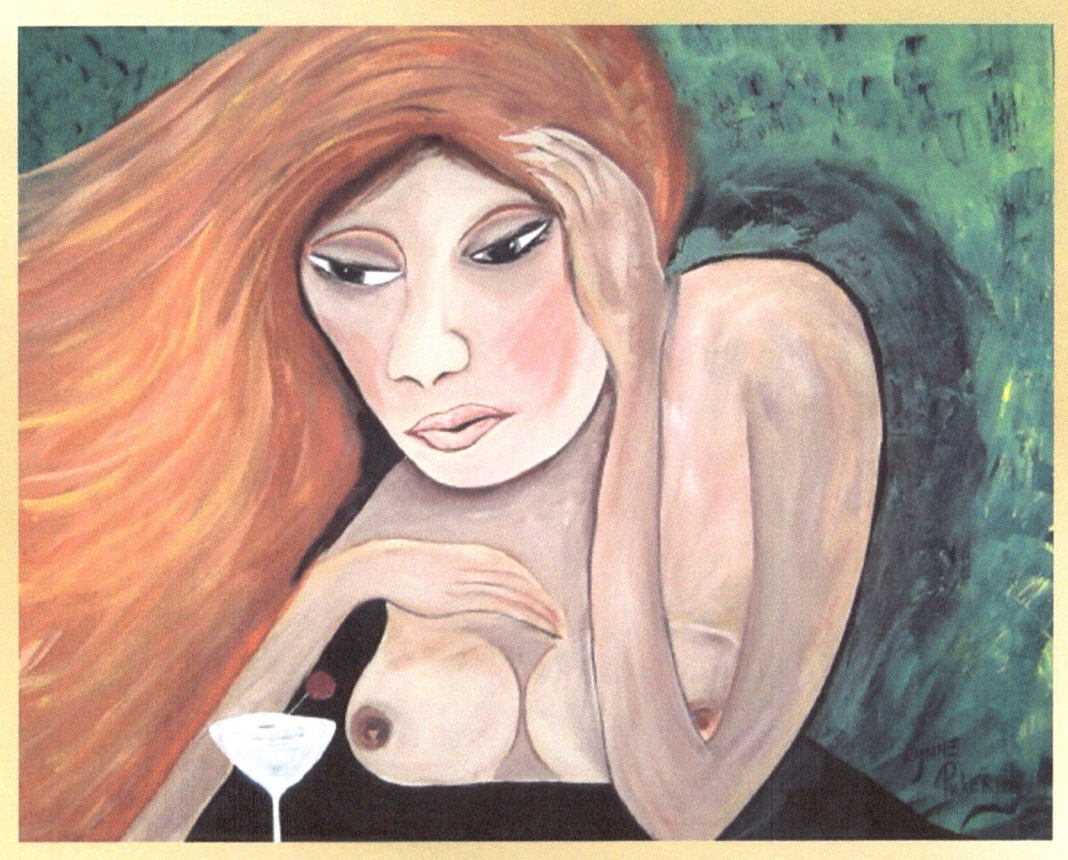

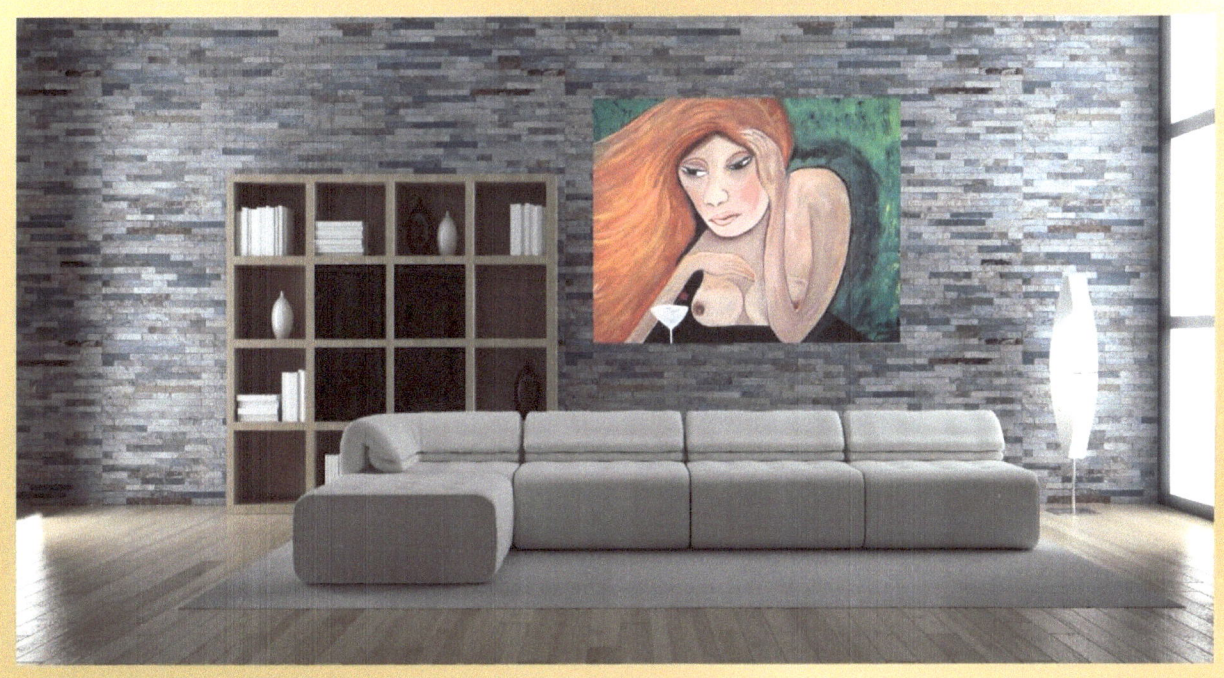

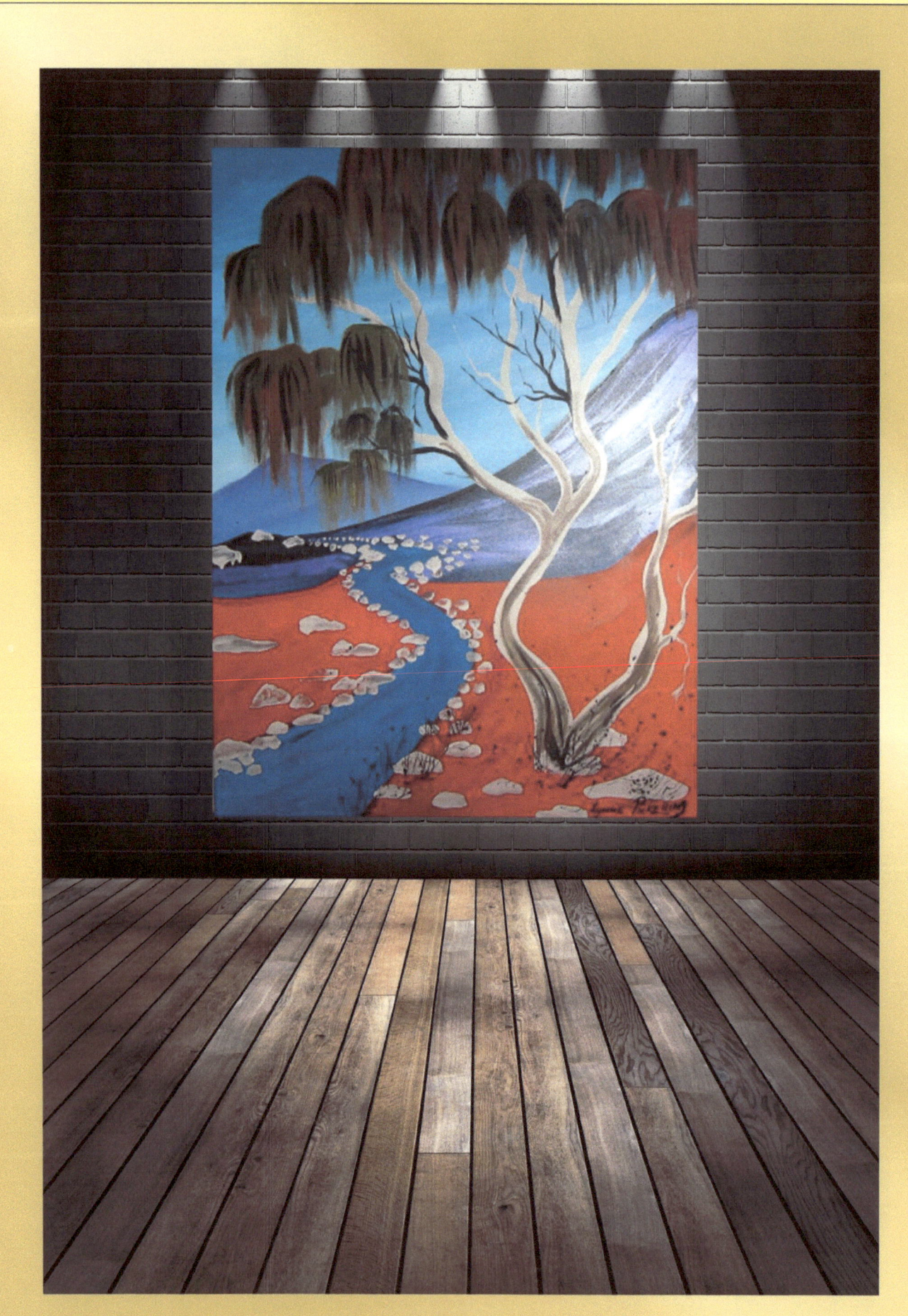

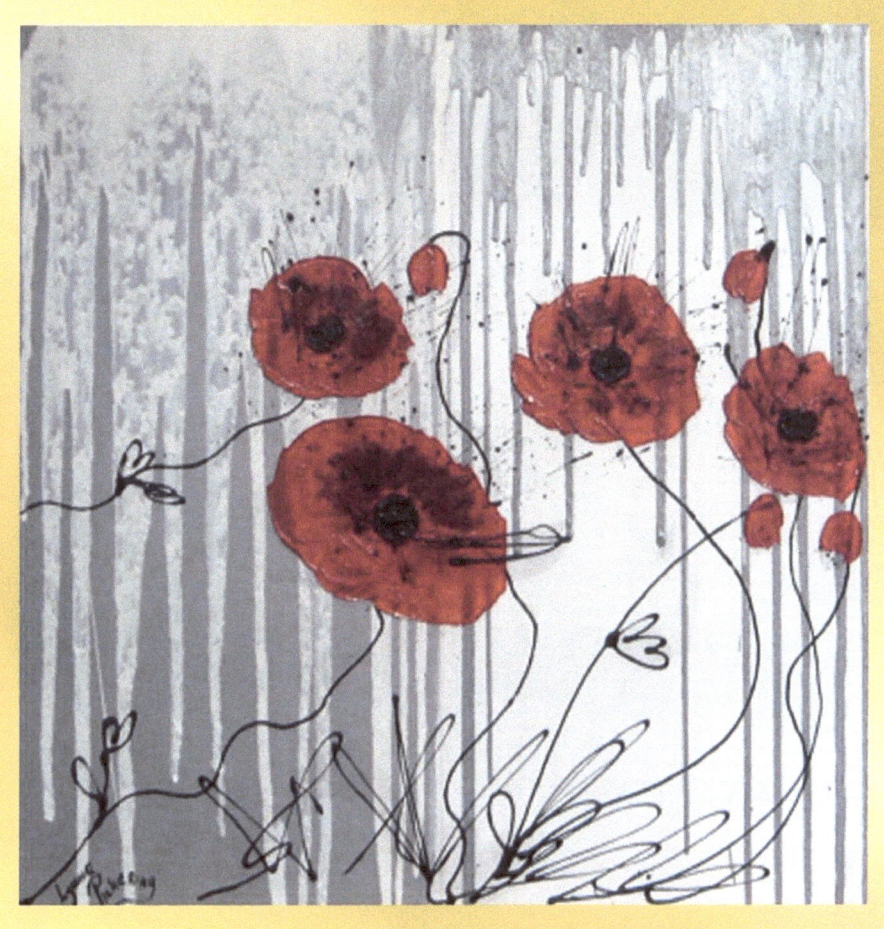

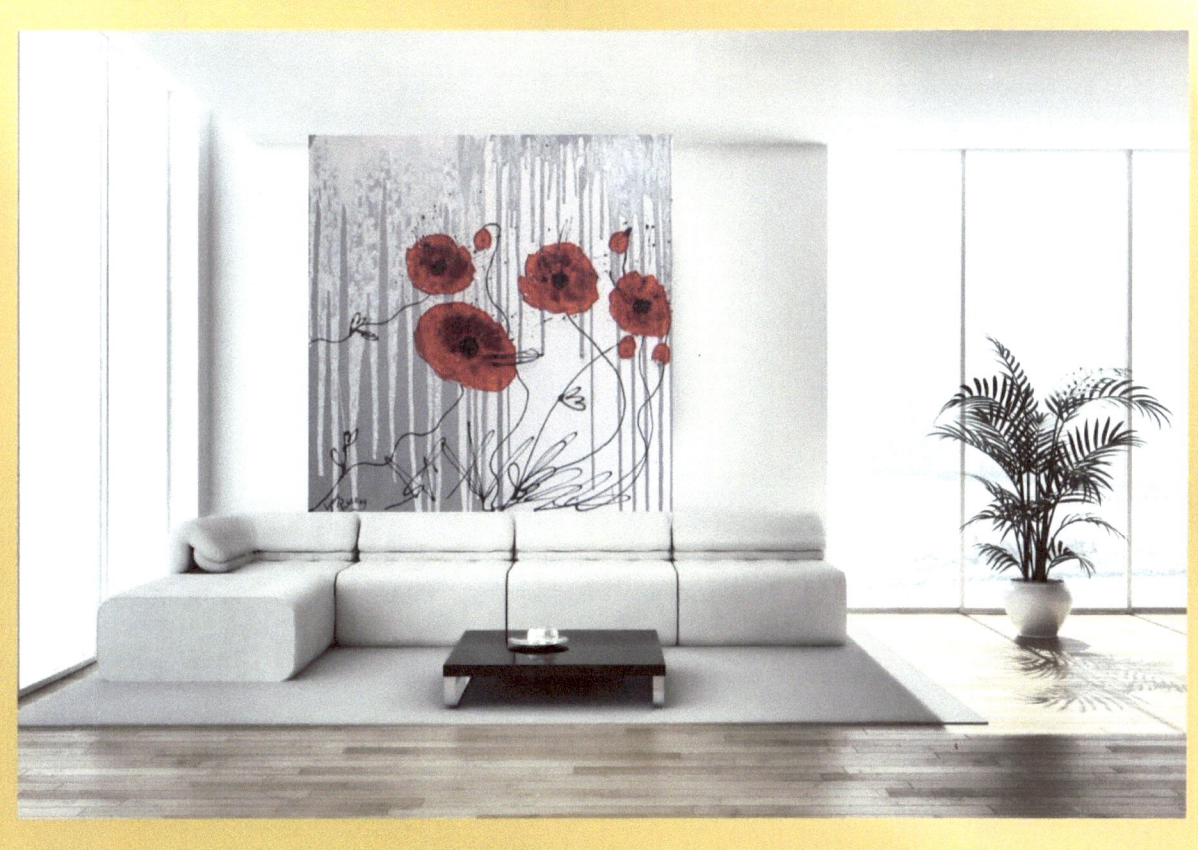

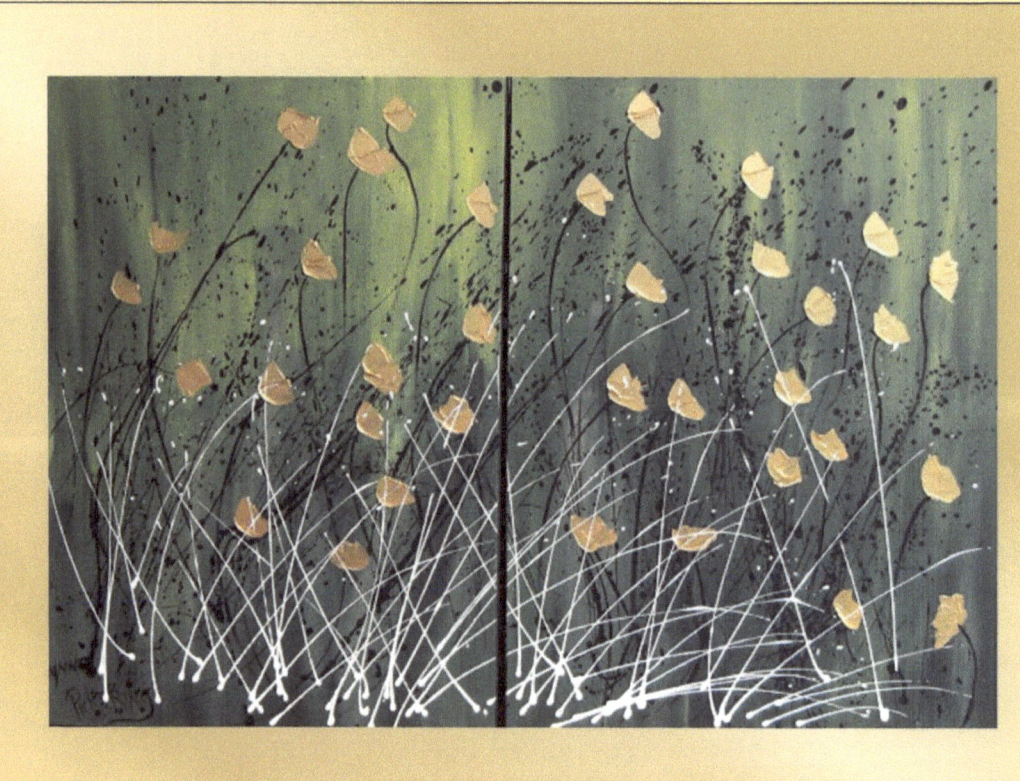

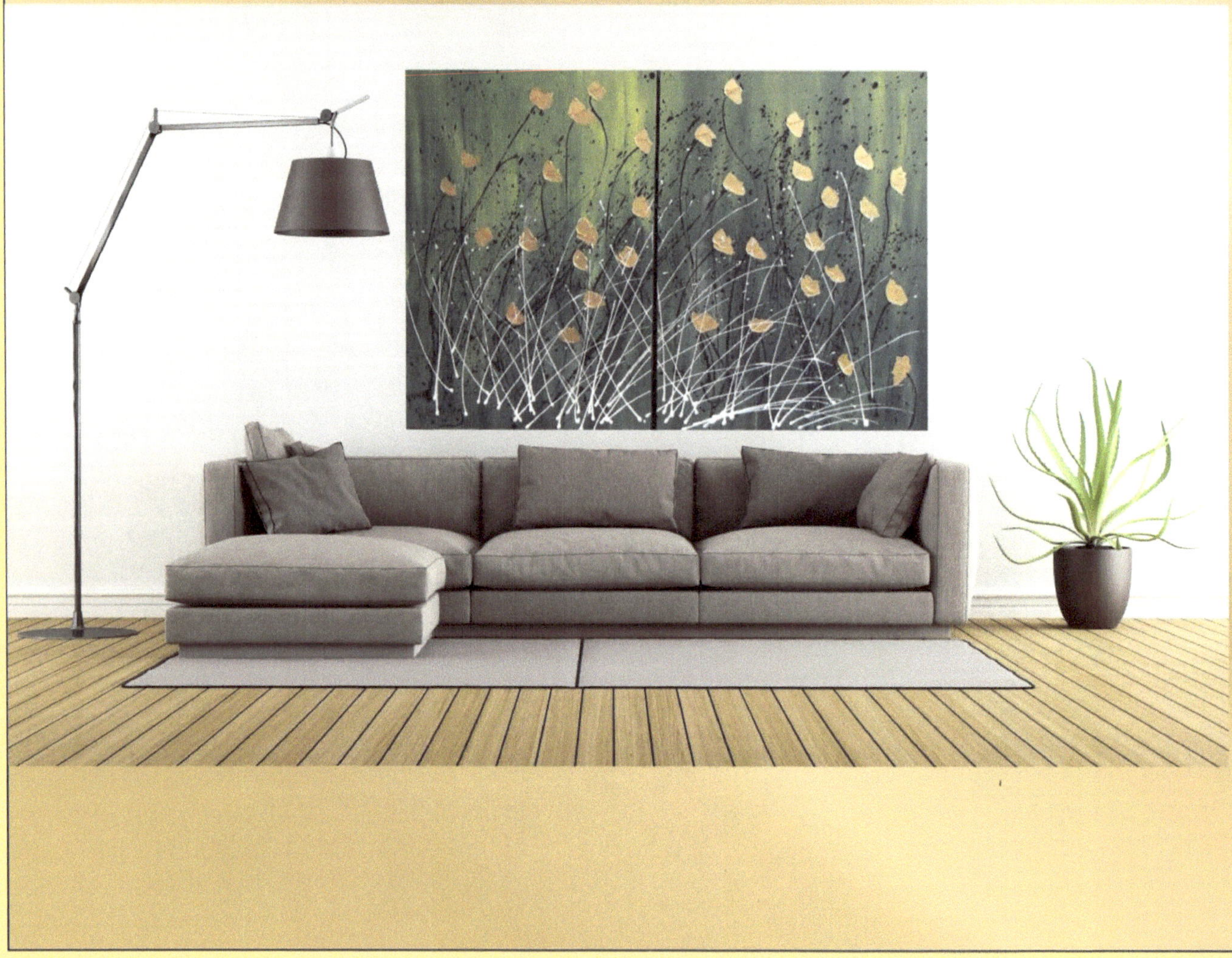

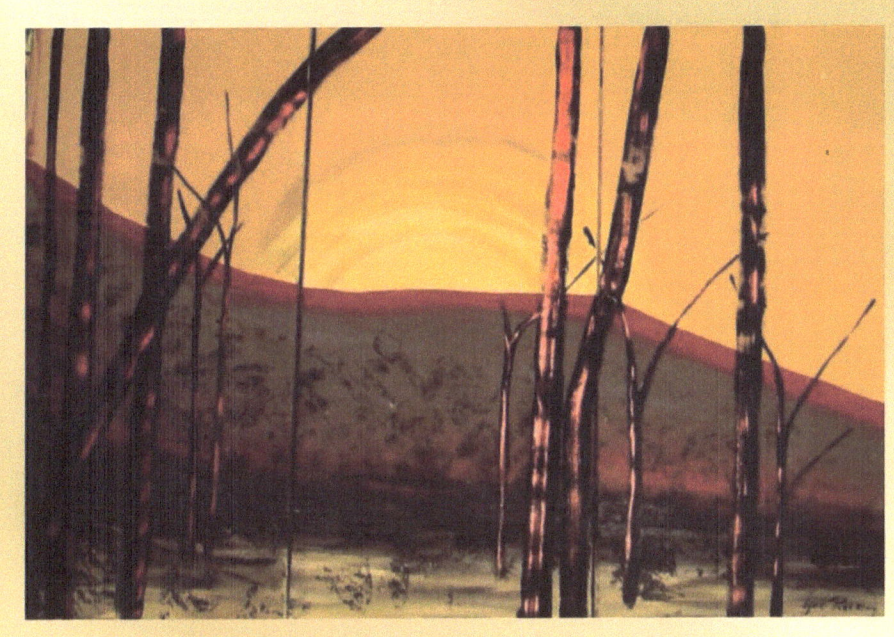

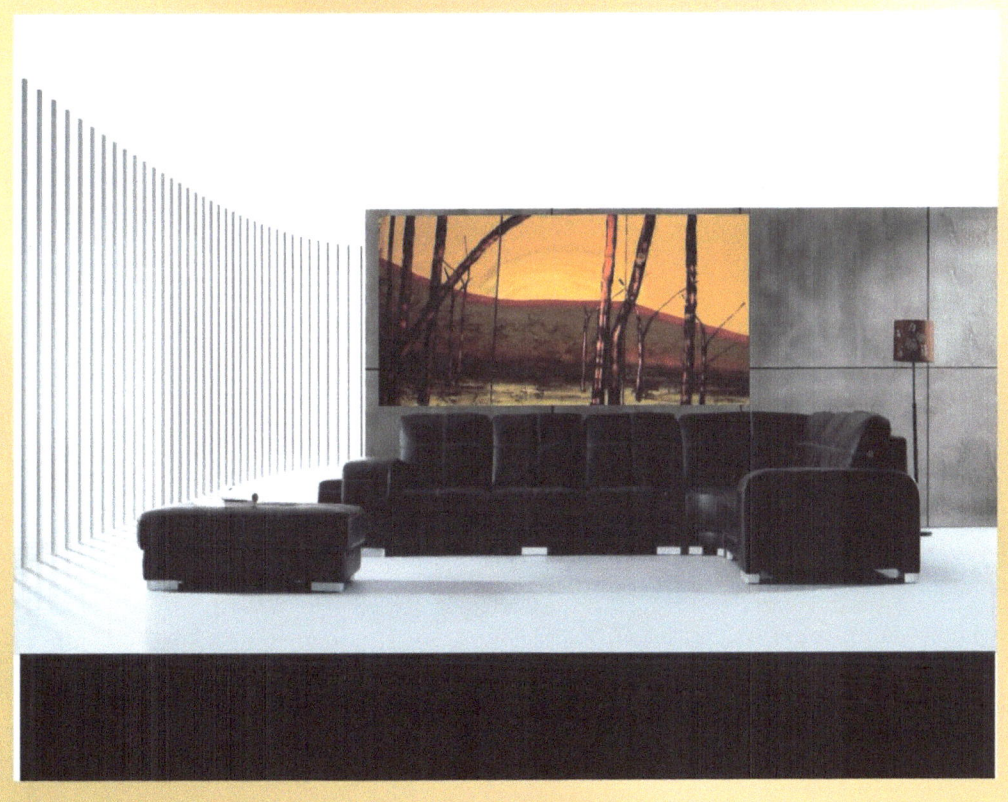

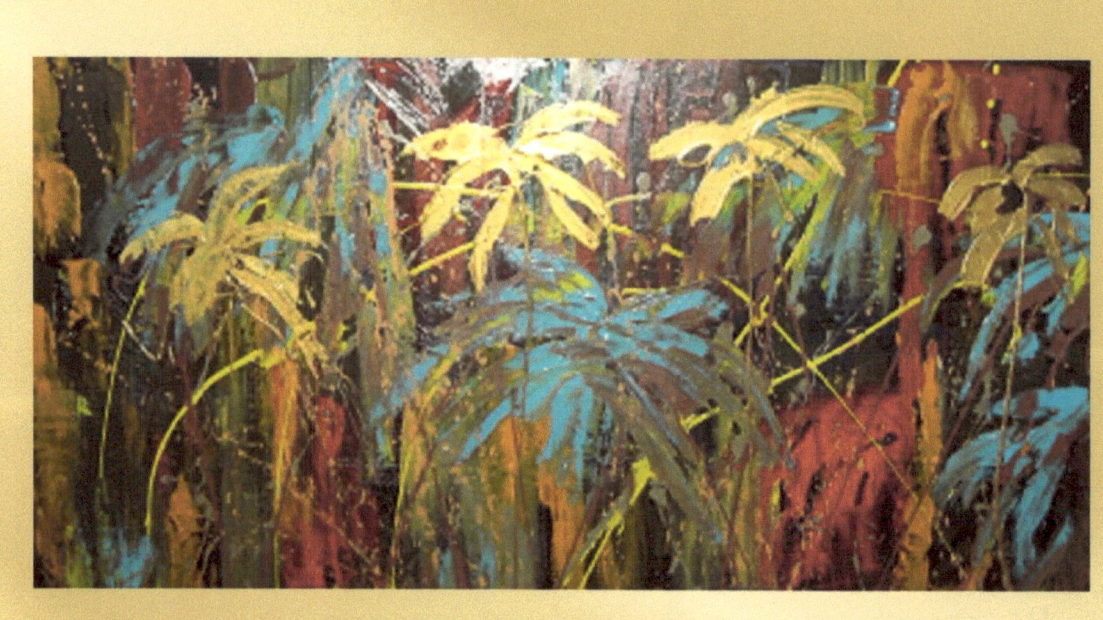

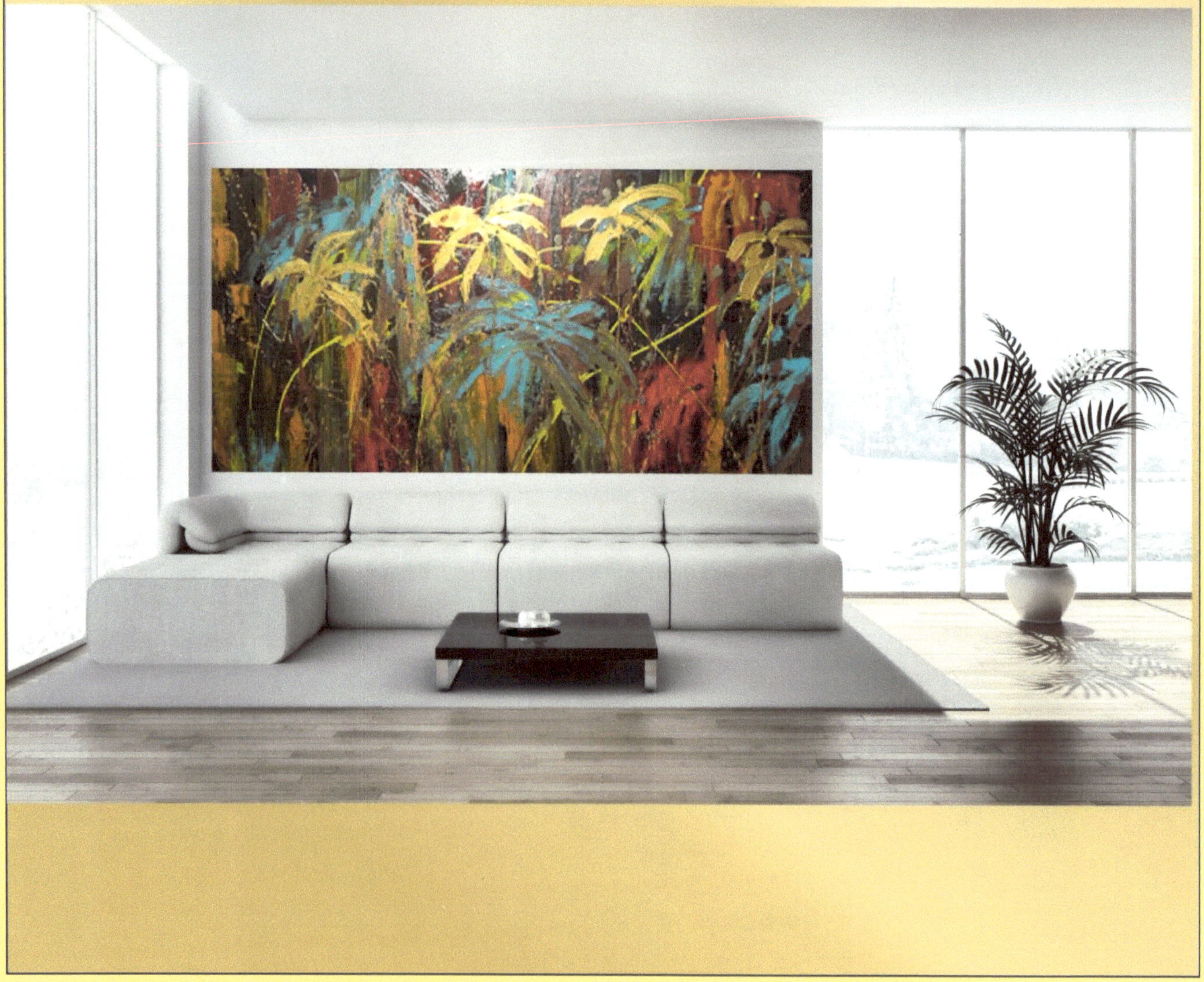

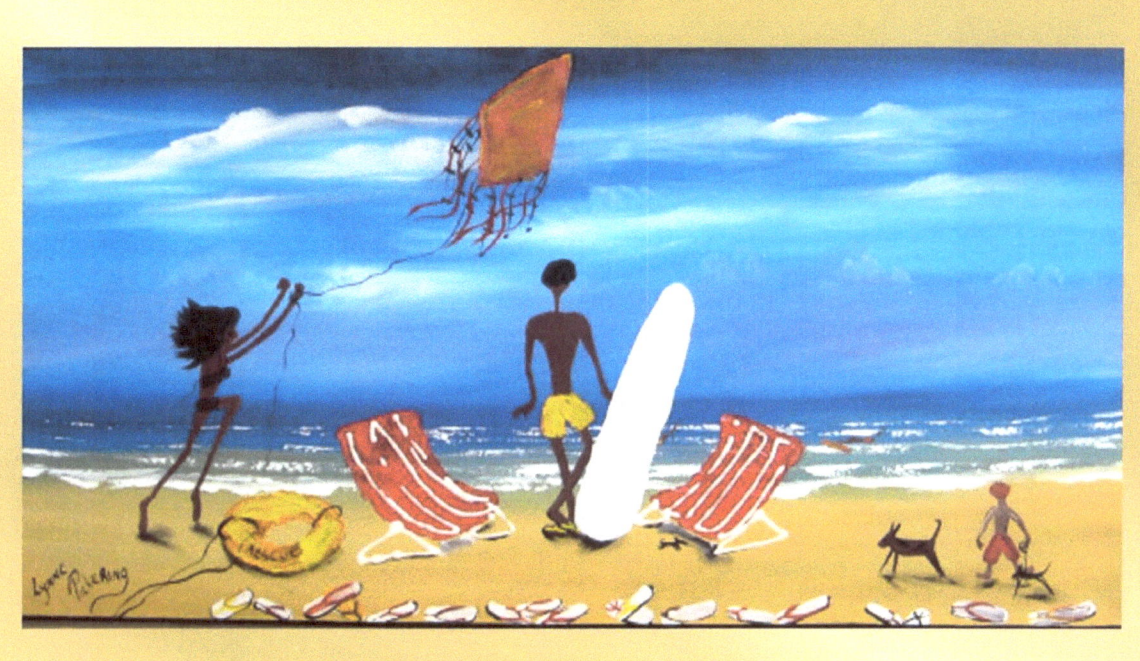

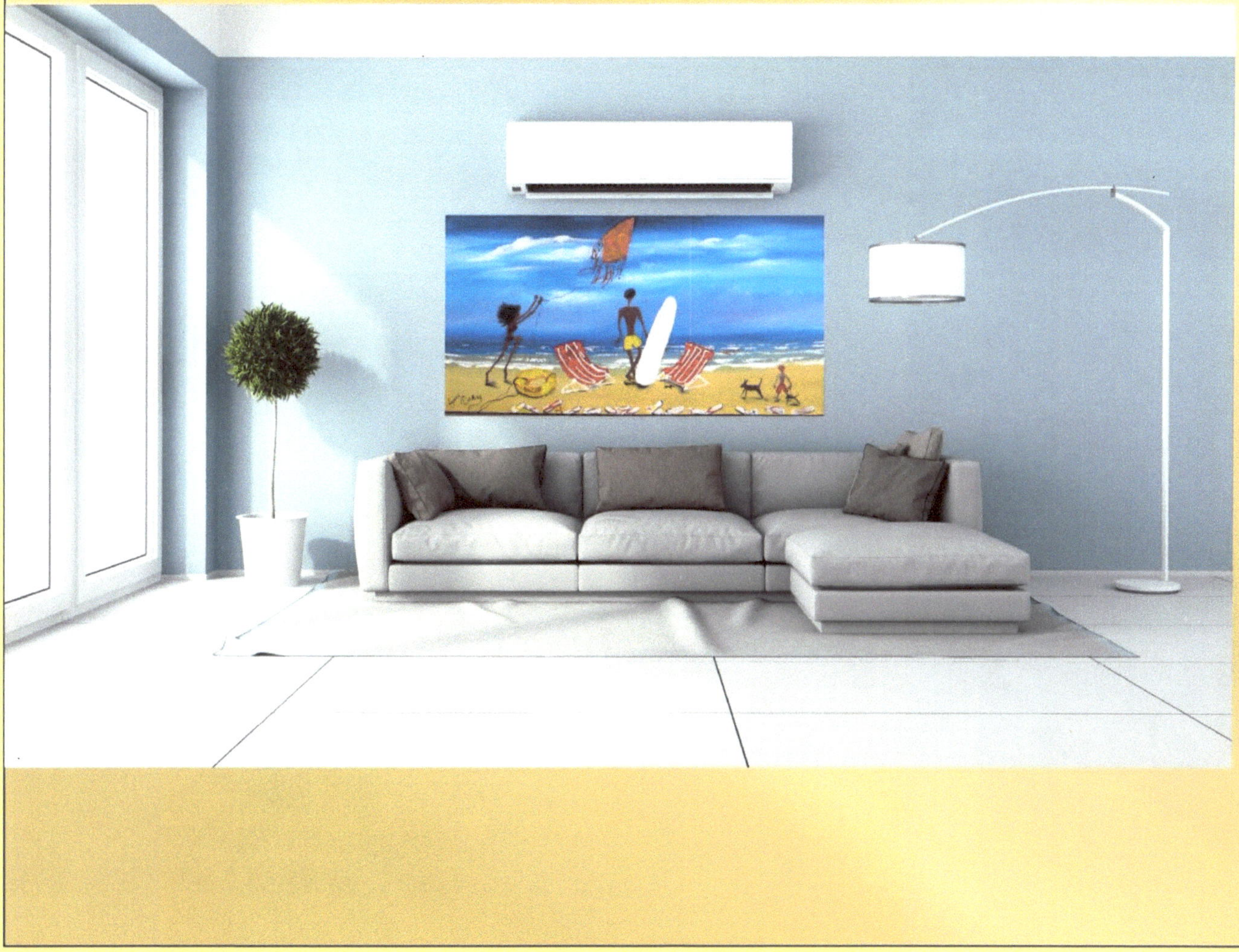

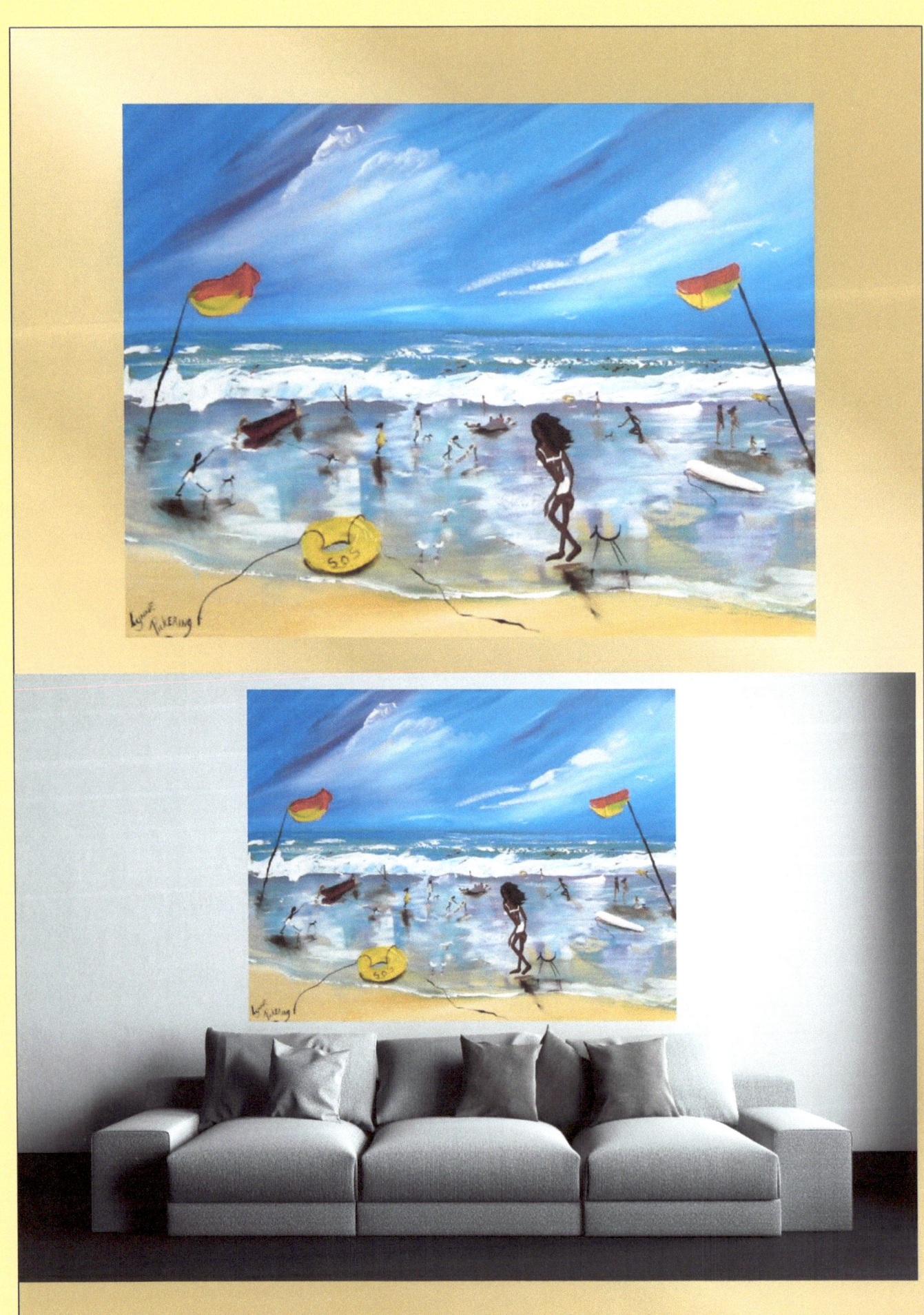

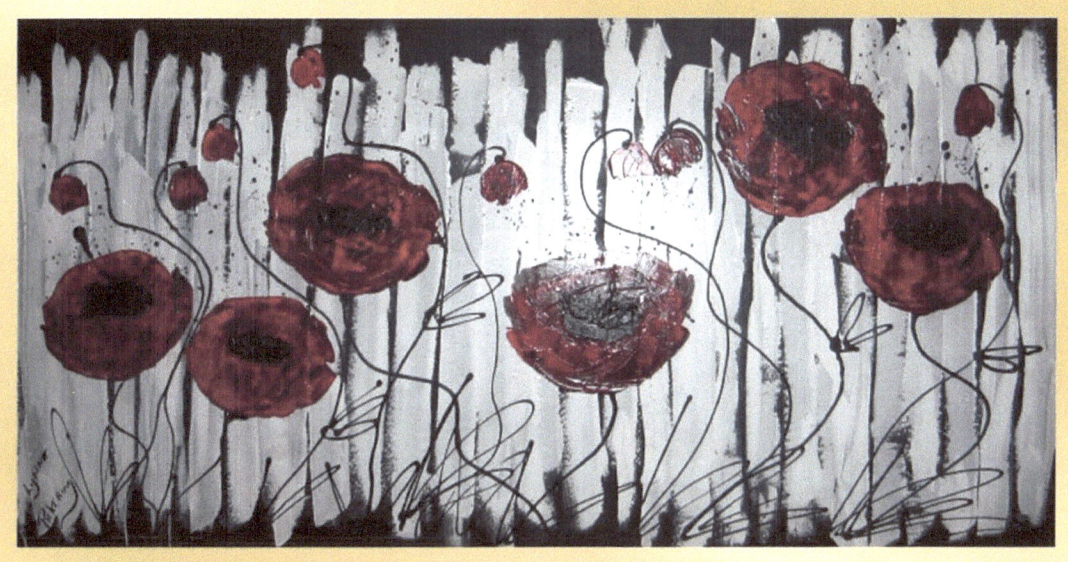

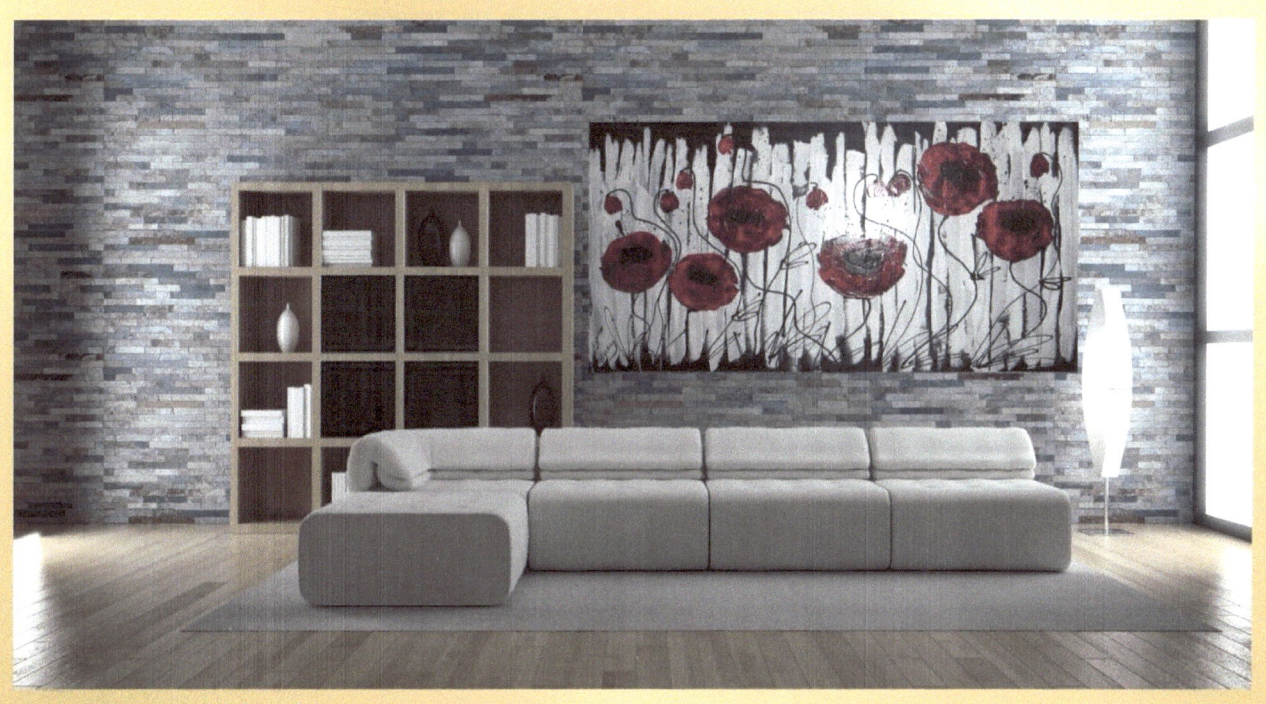